WALK WITH THE PEOPLE

WALK
with the
PEOPLE

LATINO MINISTRY IN THE
UNITED STATES

Juan Francisco Martínez

Abingdon Press
Nashville

WALK WITH THE PEOPLE
LATINO MINISTRY IN THE UNITED STATES

Copyright © 2008 by Abingdon Press

All rights reserved.

This book is printed on acid-free paper.

Library of Congress Cataloging-in-Publication Data

Martinez, Juan Francisco, 1957-
Walk with the people : Latino ministry in the United States / Juan Francisco Martinez.
    p. cm.
Includes bibliographical references (p.   ).
ISBN 978-0-687-64719-4 (binding: pbk., adhesive - perfect : alk. paper)
1. Church work with Hispanic Americans.   2. Hispanic American Protestants—Religious life.
I. Title.

BV4468.2.H57M37 2008
277.3'08308968—dc222

                                                                                    2008028158

All scripture quotations unless noted otherwise are taken from New Revised Standard Version of the Bible, copyright 1989, Division of Christian Education of the National Council of the Churches of Christ in the United States of America. Used by permission. All rights reserved.

"Hay una senda," lyrics by Robert C. Savage, appears by permission of Brentwood-Benson Music Publishing, © 1960 Singspiration Music.

08 09 10 11 12 13 14 15 16 17—10 9 8 7 6 5 4 3 2 1

MANUFACTURED IN THE UNITED STATES OF AMERICA

Contents

Charts and Diagrams

Introduction

During the early twenty-first century, Latinos became the largest minority group in the United States. We are younger than the population at large, we have a higher birth rate, and we are the group with the largest number of new immigrants, both legal and undocumented, in the United States. Everything seems to indicate that soon there will be more Latinos in California than "Anglos" and that our presence in other states will continue to grow. Nonetheless, we are a very diverse group and we are becoming more diversified as we continue growing.

Various studies of the Latino community have also demonstrated that we are having an impact on religious life in the United States. Latinos make up more than a third of all US Catholics and more than half of the parishioners in many Catholic churches. The number of Latinos who identify themselves as Protestants is also growing, particularly among Pentecostals. Every day there are more Latino Protestant churches in the United States and also more Latinos in churches that are part of majority culture.

Our growth and our religious impact represent a series of very specific challenges for pastors and leaders who minister in the Latino community. *Walk with the People* was written for them. This book identifies and analyzes the contemporary challenges facing Latino *evangélico* churches in the United States and some of the challenges they are likely to encounter in the future. Latino pastors, and others who minister in the community, need to understand and address these issues. As the Latino community continues growing and diversifying,

9

effective leaders in the Latino community will reorient their ministries to respond to these changes.

Walk with the People begins with a description of some of the challenges the Latino community faces. The first chapter reviews the principal differences that exist among us; historical, national, cultural, racial, linguistic, and those related to assimilation and cultural adaptation in the United States. It also analyzes the effect of globalization, migration, and the encounter with other minority groups on the Latino community.

Chapter 2 describes how US Protestant churches have dealt with these challenges. It includes a short analysis of the various ways Protestant churches and denominations have responded to the specific pastoral realities of the Latino community. The chapter concludes by describing some of the challenges of being both Latino and Protestant in the mainstream denominations of the United States.

The third chapter begins by questioning the deficiency model than is often used to define ministry in the Latino community. This model focuses on what Latinos supposedly cannot do. *Walk with the People* invites the reader to change perspective. It assumes that Latinos have many useful resources for the task before us. This chapter describes some of those resources and various ways that Latino leaders, and others, can use them to address the pastoral needs of the community. Latinos have strong extended families, strong faith in God, and a *mestizaje* [cultural, ethnic, or racial mixes] that provides us with flexible cultural models. Also, the majority of Latino *evangélico* churches, particularly in urban areas, are multicultural and are committed to ministry among the marginalized of US society. These resources are indispensible for Latino *evangélico* churches as they address present and future challenges in the Latino community.

The second half of the book describes how Latino churches are addressing the challenges, using the strengths that we bring to the task. Chapter 4 describes how Latino Protestants are working in the community at the moment. There are multiple models of churches and ministries that are addressing the

10

challenges and opportunities described in earlier chapters. Some of these models are based in majority culture churches, while others are based in Latino churches. This chapter examines the existing models and focuses on ways to develop ministry models that are flexible, multicultural, interdependent, and able to respond to the various aspects of the Latino community.

Chapter 5 focuses on the future in various ways. It deals with some of the specific challenges of ministering to Latino youth. This chapter also delineates some of the specific responsibilities of preparing a new generation of Latino leaders for tomorrow's church. It also follows another track, describing new church and ministry models that are in formative stages and that need to be taken into account as the Latino community continues diversifying. Here Latino leaders are invited to work from within the Latino community to develop a vision that extends beyond the community. This chapter ends by recognizing the existence of undefined variables that will affect the future of Latinos in the United States. Each of these variables can affect the growth of the community and its impact on this country. Therefore, as Latino *evangélico* leaders dream and plan for the future, they will need both analytical tools to interpret the changes as they occur and a broad vision in order to walk toward the future.

The last chapter presents various analogies and images to orient ministries based in Latino reality so that Latino leaders can serve effectively in this growing diversity that is our community. The hope is that these analogies can serve as the basis for dreaming about what might be the flashes of God's future that Latinos represent in the United States.

Throughout the book I have included the perspectives and commentaries of Latino pastors and leaders who are involved in various aspects of ministry in the community. I sought to include a large variety of the differences that exist among Latinos. These leaders offer different perspectives on ministry; are from different theological traditions; and have multigenerational perspectives, different national backgrounds, and different perspectives on the role Latinos should play in US

11

society. What they have in common is a commitment to serve within the Latino community. I want to take this moment to thank all those who completed questionnaires or participated in interviews, making this part of the book possible.[1]

I am interested in Latino ministry for many reasons. I am a fifth-generation Latino *evangélico* and the son of Latino pastors. I have been a pastor and church planter and I worked in Guatemala for nine years preparing Central American leaders for ministry. I now direct a program at Fuller Theological Seminary that prepares Latino leaders for ministry in the United States. This book was born from my experience as a pastor, a supervisor of pastors, and a person who prepares others for ministry.

But the initial motivation for the book came out of a class I teach at Fuller Seminary, *Iglesias evangélicas latinas—Retos para el futuro* (Latino *Evangélico* Churches—Challenges for the Future). Most of the students who have taken this course have been pastors who are ministering in the midst of the complexities described in this book. These students have helped me broaden my understanding of ministry in the Latino community, and some read a preliminary version of the book. That is why I want to thank the generations of students that have been a part of the development of this course and, indirectly, of this book.

Walk with the People is written from a Latino Protestant perspective because that is my background and these are my people. Occasionally I mention some of the historical tensions between Latino Catholics and Protestants because these have implications for ministry in the Latino community. Nonetheless, the book represents a Protestant vision of ministry among Latinas and reflects this way of understanding pastoral work in the community.

The community I am addressing does not have a single name that identifies us all. We are part of Protestant Christianity, but the great majority of Latino Protestants have not described ourselves as *"protestantes."* In some parts of the Spanish-speaking world *"cristiano"* is used to describe Protestants and *"católico"* is used for Catholics. This usage is common even among

12

Catholics, though it seems to deny that we are all part of the Christian tradition.

I use the word *evangélico* as almost synonymous of *Protestant* and not as a translation of *evangelical* in English.[2] I do not wish to lose this broader use of the term, though I recognize the complexities of its usage in the United States and parts of Latin America. In this book I will be using *evangélico* in this broader sense. Therefore, I will use *evangélico* in Spanish to refer to the Latino Protestant community and not only to the segment of the community identified with the US *evangelical* movement. To avoid confusion I will use *evangelical* to refer to churches, movements, or people that are identified with the common US English usage of the term.

I also recognize the "sexist" and "machista" difficulties of using some terms from Spanish, such as Latino and *evangélico*.[3] There are many solutions to this problem. In the English edition I have chosen to use both masculine and feminine terms (*evangélicos* or *evangélicas*) when referring to the group (people or community) and to interchange the masculine and feminine when referring to individuals (Latinos or Latinas) if there is no direct reference to gender. I realize that this "solution" creates its own problems and that some will not feel fully comfortable with this style. Nonetheless, it will likely be *mañana* before we find a solution that both respects the conventions of the Spanish language and does not exclude half of the population. Until that day I ask both women and men to see themselves included in the masculine and feminine references.

A particular focus of this book is that it addresses Latinos as subjects, as agents of ministry. I write from within the Latino community, principally to Latino pastors and leaders and others committed to working among Latinos. Since the goal is that all Latino leaders have access to this book, it is being published simultaneously in English and Spanish. I am grateful to Abingdon Press and particularly to Robert Ratcliff, Emanuel Vargas, and Pedro Lopez for all their work in making this bilingual publication possible.

At the end of *Walk with the People*, there is a short list of resources for those who wish to analyze more deeply some of

13

the topics addressed in the book. It is not meant to be exhaustive in relationship to the types of ministry resources available in the Latino community. Nonetheless, it includes information about how to access a broader resource base.

We live and minister in the midst of many complexities. We are part of a globalized world, and Latinos are in constant movement in many directions between North and South, within the United States, and around the world. We are encountering people from all over the world, something which is changing the very definition of what it means to call oneself Latina. We have been the object of Catholic and Protestant mission in the United States for over 150 years. Our experiences in the United States have left us with polycentric identities. We are also living and serving in the midst of other profound political, social, economic, and religious changes. *Walk with the People* was written for my sisters and brothers who are serving in this context with a strong commitment and a profound sense of God's call. My prayer is that it will provide insight and tools so that they might minister more effectively in this place and in this time in which God calls us to a *kairos* moment.

Juan Francisco Martínez
Los Angeles, California
September 2008

14

1

The Complexities of Our Latina Reality

On Plaza Olvera in Los Angeles one can buy tee shirts that say things like "I am Chicano, not Hispanic." On the other hand, a friend who recently arrived in the United States was lamenting: "I have been an Argentinian all my life. Now I am in the United States and they tell me I am Latino. I have never been Latino and I really do not understand what that is." These two examples reflect the complexity of Latino identity. We use terms like *Latino* or *Hispanic* to describe ourselves and some of us insist on one or the other. Many among us reject both of the terms and do not understand why we are identified as Latinos or Hispanics and not by terms that identify our specific national backgrounds.

The United States Census Bureau and government offices began using the term *Hispanic* to identify "the Hispanic" peoples in 1970. Since that date Hispanic has been used as a category next to the "racial" categories of white, Asian American, African American, and other similar categories. Hispanic is neither a racial, ethnic, national, geographic, nor linguistic category, though it includes aspects of each of these. Therefore, the Census Bureau uses a series of explanations next to the term to clarify what it means and what it does not mean and who is or is not Hispanic.

The "Hispanic/Latino" community has debated the usage of *Hispanic*, and many people prefer the term *Latino*. Many reasons are given for the preference, including that *Hispanic* identifies the community with Spain, while *Latino* identifies us with Latin America. Political and regional debates have been held with respect to each word used to identify Latinos in the United States. The debate reflects the complexity of the people that one wants to identify with the terms.[1]

Both *Latino* and *Hispanic* are terms that define the unity of various US communities that have ties to Latin America or with the Spanish-speaking world. They serve as a type of umbrella that focuses on what unites us, but they also mask a whole series of differences among those called *Latinos*. Ministry among Latinos is done in the space between the unity and the multiple differences among our people.[2]

Our Identities

There are many types of national, ethnic, racial, and cultural distinctions among Latinos. One of the most common ways to define those differences is by means of our national backgrounds. According to the US Census Bureau, Latinos have the following national backgrounds:

Mexicans and Mexican-Americans	65.9%
Puerto Ricans	9.5%
Central Americans	7.8%
South Americans	5.2%
Cubans	4.0%
Other Latino groups	7.6%[3]

This way of describing our differences places the emphasis on our histories and on the national and cultural influences that formed us. If we describe Latinas this way, we notice several geographic and demographic tendencies among Latinos. For example, Mexicans and Mexican-Americans are concentrated in the Southwest, Puerto Ricans and Dominicans in the Northeast, and Cubans in southern Florida.[4] Defining our-

16

selves by our national backgrounds helps us identify how and when we became a part of the United States and helps recognize the cultural differences that formed us.[5]

This type of distinction takes our national backgrounds into account, but hides the differences within those backgrounds. Many "minorities" within the Latina minority become invisible in this description. In particular, indigenous immigrants, those of African descent, those from English- or French-speaking areas, those who come from immigrant communities that have maintained their previous national identities, or those who were recent immigrants to Latin America before coming to the United States.

Defining ourselves by our national backgrounds is also not useful when describing our place in the United States today. It gives the impression that all Latinas are immigrants, people who recently arrived from "outside." It does not

> Those of us who were born outside of the United States need help to understand the millions of historical factors that affect our ministries: how people feel and react when they confront specific people or situations. What is more, it is not the same to have been born in Mexico (very close to the US) than to have been born in Argentina (very far from the US).
>
> JORGE SÁNCHEZ

take into account that the first European communities in what is now the United States, were Spanish, not English, and that there has been "Hispanic" influence in the territorial US for centuries. This framing does not take into account the Latinos in the United States who are descendants of those who arrived in what is now the United States when it was part of Spain or Mexico. It also does not take into account the particular reality of the Puerto Ricans who have been citizens of the United States almost since this country took the island from Spain more than a century ago, but who, nonetheless, live in an "intermediate" situation, since Puerto Rico is neither an independent country, nor a state of the United States. These histories of "conquest" point toward another way of reflecting on the differences among us, our different experiences with relationship to the United States.[6]

17

Those who were in the Southwest when the United States took the land from Mexico were conquered. Puerto Ricans were colonized after the United States took the island from Spain. On the other hand, Cubans have usually been accepted as political refugees, so they have had a much more positive experience in the United States. The experience of other immigrants has varied, many times depending on educational background and the color of one's skin. The person who arrived in the United States with a visa has a very different perspective than the one who arrived as an undocumented alien. Persons with a European background report different experiences from those with African, Asian, indigenous, or *mestizo* backgrounds. That is why many Latinas see this country as a land of great opportunity and acceptance while others have more negative or ambivalent perspectives. And we must not overlook the complexity of the undocumented persons who come to this country hoping for new opportunities, but who live in the shadows of US reality and in fear of legal officials.

One more very important factor defines us and makes our differences stand out. This has to do with the level of identification with Latino culture and the level of adaptation and assimilation to majority culture in this country or the level of encounter with other minority groups. At this point we are talking about each Latina's self-identity: how are we a part of the Latino reality in this country and how are we a part of the larger society? This factor recognizes that we are a people in process. One cannot describe Latinos statically or monoculturally (Latino or Anglo). This factor recognizes that Latinos are a people in cultural and social movement and that many of us have polycentric identities.[7]

The following diagram on page 19 can help us understand the complexity of our identities.

This diagram demonstrates that there are many things at play when we think of our Latino identity. We live under the influence of majority culture and its assimilationist tendencies. There are many things that pull us toward majority culture, including the mass media, the public schools, and direct and

18

indirect social pressure. We also recognize that everyone who lives in the United States has to adapt to majority culture at some level, even though a person might look for ways to maintain a particular ethnic identity or might live in areas with a high concentration of Latinos.

Figure 1A
Levels of identification with Latino culture

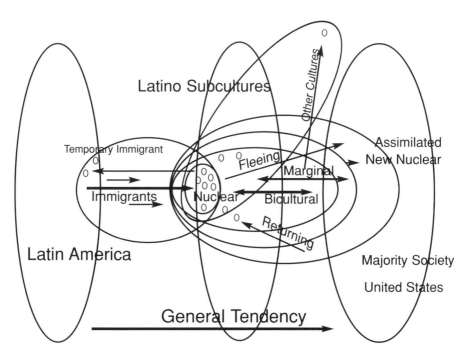

On the other hand, there are also other cultures in this country. Even though they do not have the same power of attraction as majority culture, some—in particular the African-American culture—have had a great deal of influence on US Latino culture. Some Latinos have also been drawn by some of the other cultural expressions one finds in this country.

Certain factors strengthen Latina culture, such as history, migration, Spanish mass media, and the size of the community. But we recognize that Latino identity is polycentric and fluid. There seems to be some space in which Latinas can opt for the **19** level of identification they want to have with their background. Within this space and these influences, we can identify various levels of identification with Latino culture and with majority culture.

In the first place, one finds *nuclear* Latinos. These are people who live almost completely within their Latino community and have very limited contact with majority culture. Many times these people are recent immigrants or people who migrated when they were older adults. The majority of these people speak Spanish as their principal or only language.

Generally, one assumes that nuclear Latinos are recent immigrants from Latin America who only speak Spanish and live in Latino barrios. But there is also a significant group of Latinos who fit in this category, even though they speak little Spanish or only speak English. These are people who live in areas of high Latino population density (such as south Texas, northern New Mexico, the agricultural communities of central California or parts of Los Angeles, New York, Miami, or Chicago) and who were raised and live their lives in Latino communities. Their culture is not Latin American, but it is also not "Anglo." These communities reflect cultural adaptation to US society, but they also maintain strong, distinctive Latino traits and many are strengthened by new immigrants.

A second type is a *bicultural* Latino. This person lives his life negotiating between majority culture and the Latino community. He understands the cultural "rules" of each group, can fit in either, and chooses to maintain a balance between both in his being, almost always, in some level of tension. The majority of these people were born or raised in the United States. Generally, they are fully bilingual and can speak both languages without an "accent." They live different aspects of their lives in each of the two worlds, though sometimes they do not fully feel comfortable in either.

There are also bicultural Latinas who learn to live between Latino culture and another minority culture. What was said in the previous paragraph applies to them, but in relationship to another minority group in this country.

20

The *Marginal* Latino makes up a third type of identification. This person has not disconnected herself from Latino culture, but she only identifies with it in an occasional manner. She likes some of the Latino cultural artifacts (food, music, soap operas) and enjoys spending time in the Latino community, but she lives her life according to the patterns of majority culture (or another culture). Some Latinos who were raised in Latino Protestant churches continue participating in them as a way of maintaining ties to the community, even though their identification with other aspects of Latino culture is marginal.

The Latino who is *fleeing* from his culture is a fourth type. This person is actively trying to be a part of majority culture and is sure that the best way to

> We have young people (second generation) born here and many feel more comfortable using English. Nonetheless, many in the "third generation" want to recover Spanish.
> FERNANDO SANTILLANA

do it is by disconnecting from anything Latino. Some refuse to speak Spanish or to relate to other Latinos. Others attempt to deny their Latino roots by "Anglosizing" their names. Even though they may not deny their past, they see it as part of the past and as a burden in this country. Their desire and goal is to incorporate into US culture as soon as possible.

The Latino who is *returning* represents a fifth type of Latino identification. These persons, often from the second, third, or fourth generation, rediscover their Latino identity and seek to strengthen it. Some were raised within majority culture but now want to reclaim aspects of their Latino identity. One sees this tendency among Latino young people who are attempting to find their place as Latinos and as part of the United States. Another type that returns has "succeeded" in majority culture but feels that he has lost part of his identity and is seeking to recuperate it.

Assimilated Latinos are a sixth type. These persons identify as Hispanic or Latino when reporting to the US Census Bureau, but their cultural expressions and lifestyle are completely of majority culture. They do not have significant Latino cultural **21** features, only a historical memory that their ancestors were from Latin America or the Spanish-speaking world. They do not feel identified with the Latino community and reflect the "success" of the assimilating effort of US society.

There is still a seventh option, that of the Latino who becomes a part of *another culture*. This person is leaving behind her Latino background and assimilating, not into majority culture, but into another minority culture, many times by marriage. For example, there are Latinos who are not only attracted to African-American culture but are identifying themselves completely with it.[8]

What this drawing cannot illustrate is how dynamic an impact this encounter between cultures really is and how it affects people. "Anglo" culture is dominant in this country and it seeks to assimilate those from other cultures. Anglo culture has many resources at its disposal to fulfill this task. Nonetheless, Latino culture also has an impact, though small, on the dominant culture. Other cultural expressions are also participating in this process. In this encounter between live and elastic cultures, one sees a process of constant change, change that has an impact on each culture.

This process of encounter affects the members of each culture, creating changes in all of the cultures that are part of the process, though minority cultures are more affected. Latinos find themselves in the midst of a process of adaptation and under pressure to assimilate. But we are also culture creators and are adapting our culture to the reality of living in the United States. This process of adaptation can be seen in the dynamic of the various levels of identification just described. This process is not static or unidirectional. Latinos move within this process in different ways and directions at different points in their lives. A nuclear Latino might opt to leave his subculture and an assimilated Latina might rediscover her *latinidad*. Latino young people might experiment with various options as they define their identity. It is in the midst of this process, and with people at various levels of identification, that Latino culture continues to develop.

Another aspect that is difficult to show in a diagram is the process of new cultural creations that are developing in the globalized cultural encounter. One sees cultural expressions that are drawing from various cultures and are creating new spaces and identities. It is yet to be seen which of these expressions will be considered variants of existing cultures and which will need new names to distinguish them from existing cultures.

If one takes into account the assimilationist pressure of the United States and the fact of acculturation and social assimilation of many Latinos, one needs to explain how it is that there continues to be a clearly definable Latino community today. This is due to several important factors: (1) the historical relationship between the United States and Latin America, (2) the proximity of the United States to Mexico and Latin America, (3) the constant migration from Spanish-speaking countries, and (4) the existence of large Latino communities (cultural hinterlands) in the United States. Because of these factors, Latino culture and the Spanish language continue to gain strength, in spite of the assimilationist influence of US majority culture and the growing number of Latinos who have fully assimilated into majority culture or into other cultures.

One notices certain generational tendencies in the level of ethnic identity and many speak of first- and second- (or later) generation Latinos as a way of describing the changes of acculturation and assimilation. There is a certain reality behind this observation, though it does not sufficiently explain the Latino experience. In areas of high Latino concentration, there are people who are fifth- or sixth-generation who continue living in a Latino subculture and there are multigenerational Latinos in this country who continue speaking Spanish. It is also becoming more common to see US-born Latinos marrying Latina immigrants, altering the assimilation "process." Because of the constant movement of people between Latin America and the United States, Latin American influence continues in US Latino communities; and both the Spanish language and Latino culture are alive and well. So even as many individuals continue assimilating, the place and importance of Latino culture and the Spanish language continues to grow.

23

Migration, Globalization, and Identity[9]

Más allá de México

Aunque en esta vida
Yo tenga tristeza
Se que allá en el norte
Tengo una mansión.

Migration has been a part of Latino identity since 1848. During the nineteenth century, there was constant movement, in both directions, between Mexico, the Caribbean, and the United States. The flow was small, but it served as a link between communities in the United States and the Spanish-speaking world. This bidirectional pattern faced its first major change with the beginning of the Mexican Revolution in 1910. Thousands of Mexicans entered the United States fleeing the violence. This coincided somewhat with the United States' entry into World War I. Therefore, these immigrants were welcomed as workers who could take the place of the soldiers who had left the fields and the factories without laborers. In the 1930s, during the Great Depression, there was a strong anti-immigrant reaction that resulted in the deportation of many people, including people born in the United States. When World War II began, Mexican labor was sought once again; and when the war ended, there was another anti-migratory reaction. These movements began a labor and migratory pattern that continues to this day and helps explain the large number of Latinos of Mexican background. The swings in interest and rejection toward immigrant Latino labor is reflected in industries like agriculture, construction, and the service industries (janitorial, care of the infirm, food) that depend on Latino

24

labor, with or without legal documentation, and at the same time, the strong anti-immigrant stance of other segments of the US population.

Each of the Latino communities in the United States has its own migratory patterns. Puerto Ricans were declared US citizens in 1917, in part to draft them into the military. After serving in World War II, many Puerto Rican soldiers saw that there was much more economic opportunity in the United States than on the island, and in 1945 a migratory pattern between the island and some northeastern states began, a pattern that remains to this day.

Cubans began arriving in significant numbers after Fidel Castro took over power in Cuba in 1959. Throughout the years there have been several migratory waves from that island. To this day most any Cuban that arrives on US soil can remain in the country legally.

> To minister in an immigrant community, we have to know from the beginning that we will have a large permanent back door.
>
> JORGE SÁNCHEZ

Dominicans began to immigrate after the US military intervened in Santo Domingo in 1963. Migration from Central America began in earnest when the civil wars in the region heated up, particularly in El Salvador and Guatemala during the 1970s and 1980s. Some of the migratory patterns from South America are also tied to specific events and particular political situations, though on a lesser scale.[10]

Migration is now a part of the reality of our globalized world. Globalization has opened new economic opportunities but has also put new economic pressures on many people. The free movement of goods and capital is also creating a movement, though not so free, of people looking for better job options and an improved lifestyle. In the last decade there has been a large migratory flow toward the United States, with or without legal documentation, and everything seems to indicate that this will continue.

This migratory wave has certain characteristics that distinguish it. On the one hand, the ease of transportation and **25** communication means that the new immigrant does not have to cut links with Latin America. She tends to create a hybrid, polycentric, identity, one that includes the country of origin and the adopted country. She continues traveling and communicating with relatives and so has a foot "there" and a foot "here." Her identity is formed in the constant encounter between her "two countries."

Several Latin American countries are also taking advantage of this migratory flow to maintain a level of economic and social stability in their countries. Places like Mexico, El Salvador, and Guatemala greatly depend on the remittances sent by their citizens in the US to relatives back home. This money is an important source of income, and migration toward the United States is also an escape valve that allows governments in several countries to avoid or minimize important socioeconomic and political tensions. The migratory flow in both directions is also creating new subcultures in Latin America that have been influenced by the temporary experience in the United States.

These migratory patterns also have a very significant impact on Latino identity in the United States. The constant flow for several generations has created what some have called the "eternal first generation." Latinos have been in the United States for generations, but we continue being identified as immigrants. The constant migratory movement, in both directions, also helps maintain strong ties between Latino communities in the United States and Latin America.

But this movement has also affected our identity in many other ways. Some feel like India María, "ni de aquí, ni de allá."[11] Others do not want to be identified with the new immigrants. Migration also puts us in contact with Latinos with whom we would have had little contact in Latin America, creating new cultural *mestizajes*, within Latino identity. Since these movements are both northward and southward, they are also having a strong impact in Latin America. All this movement leaves us between several identities, without a common vision or commitment toward a model of participation in US society.

This Latino migratory movement is happening in the midst of global migration. Latinos are encountering other immigrants from around the world. In the US Southwest this is happening in the Borderlands of significant social and cultural change and interaction. In cities like Los Angeles or New York, more than one hundred

> The socioeconomics reality of the new immigrants causes them to reside in places that have traditionally distinguished themselves for a series of social ills. These ills become the model for our young people who are searching for their identity and trying to survive in such places.
>
> ROBERTO COLÓN

languages are spoken and new cultural *mestizajes* are constantly beingcreated. These Borderlands are seen as a place of hope for many but are also places of exploitation. The global movement of peoples creates many opportunities but also many difficulties.

This migratory movement is now part of the national debate in the United States. Immigrants, both documented and undocumented, provide many economic benefits to this country; but their presence creates a series of ten-

> The complexity of Latino identity in this country is born in the ambivalence, treatment, and historical events that began in the nineteenth century and that developed particularly in the states of the Southwest.... My perspective is that anyone who wants to minister in the Latino community needs to know their history to understand their current reality.
>
> EDUARDO FONT

sions. Some fear that the Latino presence will fundamentally change the national character and identity of the United States.[12] Sometimes it seems that people in the US want the benefits of Latino immigrant labor, but that they want the people to disappear. The fear of the potential change immigrants might bring has created an anti-Latino reaction in some segments of US society. In other words, Latino identity is also affecting the national identity.

Latino Protestant churches have grown and developed in the midst of this migratory movement. Some of the younger churches "migrated" with their members. The older ones have **27** had to deal with the changes brought by the new immigrants. Many Latino churches also have to deal with the fact that their members are in constant movement and that they have multiple church ties, both in the United States and in Latin America.

Cultural Realities

In his book, *The Hispanic Condition*, author Ilan Stavans reflects on the complexities of Latino culture and identity. We are a people [or various peoples] who continue struggling with how to clearly identify ourselves. Our varied experiences leave us without a common vision of our identity in the United States. We have leaders who call us toward total assimilation, while others seek to strengthen our distinct identity. We find it difficult to define what unites us as a people. Some argue for the usage of Spanish as our common identifier, including some who hardly speak the language. Others, like Stavans, argue for Spanglish, while many Latinos only speak English. This unresolved discussion is augmented by new generations of immigrants who have their own perspectives on what the center of Latino culture or identity should be. Also, new generations of Latinos born in the United States are creating hybrid cultures that combine the various cultural realities that they are experiencing. Since our identities are in constant flux, it is difficult to imagine a scenario in which these tensions are ever "resolved." Part of our US Latino identity and culture is to live on the hyphen "-" between the multiple influences that affect our identity.[13]

We know the needs of the Latino community, not only because I am Hispanic, the same as them, but because I was also undocumented for many years, the same as them. The needs of our people are not only spiritual, but also familial, economic, physical, educational, and, of course, also related to migratory status.

RENÉ MOLINA

Socioeconomic Situation

The growth of the Latino community in the United States is creating a series of social and economic challenges. While many Latinos are finding new socioeconomic spaces and opportunities, we are also seeing a growing number of Latinos who are lagging behind in education, health, and economic levels. Some of the most pressing problems are:

- Growing numbers of broken families
- Machismo and sexism manifested in violence against women or in limited opportunities for women
- Overcrowding suffered by many Latinos in urban areas
- Latino young people who are not finishing high school
- Growing numbers of Latinos under the poverty line
- The level of suicide among Latina adolescents
- The number of Latina single mothers
- The percentage of undocumented people living in the community
- The racism within the Latino community, particularly toward the indigenous and toward those of African descent

All of these factors are adversely affecting the Latino community. While we see and celebrate the advancement of individuals, we realize that the state of the community in general is much more difficult. The unclear future of the undocumented Latinos adds another complication to this situation because it limits the educational opportunities of many Latino young people who have lived in the United States all of their lives. It also affects the limited or nonexistent access to social services confronted by many Latinos who pay taxes but cannot use those services because they are undocumented, or are not permanent residents, even though they may be in the country legally. (For more information on the current situation of the Latino community and some of the principal studies of the community, see the bibliography at the end of this book.)

29

Latino Civic Participation

> W e need to incarnate ourselves totally in the community. Their needs should be consciously in our hearts.
>
> DAVID CASTRO

Though the Latino community is the largest minority in the United States, its size is not reflected in the political life of the country. On the one hand, a significant percentage of Latinos are not US citizens, so many Latinos cannot vote. But it is also emotionally difficult for many immigrants to become US citizens, even if they qualify. Because of their polycentric identity, many continue having strong links to their countries of origin and some have even participated actively in the political life of these countries. Other Latinos maintain a dual citizenship that keeps them linked to political life in the United States and in their countries of origin.

Limited political participation is also due to other important factors. Many US-born Latinos feel the same frustration or indifference reflected in the fact that only half of the eligible US population votes. Many Latinos who are citizens question the value of participating in the electoral process, and others live in precarious economic situations in which voting does not have a high priority. Among voting Latinas one sees the differences we have already mentioned. There is a tendency to divide our vote among the principal political parties, diluting any direct impact that might come from those of us who vote. Since we do not share a common vision of the United States, or of Latino participation in the country, our vote does not tend to influence the country in a common direction.

Another fact that limits Latino political influence is the "strange" political positions of many Latinos. The vast majority agrees with conservative Republicans on issues of personal morality, such as abortion or homosexual marriage. But Latinos also have more affinity with Democrats on issues of social impact, such as immigration reform, education, and social welfare programs. This creates a difficult situation for many Latinos, who vote for one party or the other depending on which of these two major areas weigh more for them during any particular election.

All of these factors cause the Latino vote to have a much smaller impact than it could, given the size of the community. This limits the capacity of the Latino community to influence US government decisions that need to be made in response to the social problems mentioned in the previous section. As the Latino community continues to grow, so will its political influence. But it will probably be a long time before its influence corresponds to its demographic size.

Conclusion

Latino churches have the challenge of ministering in the midst of this complexity. Latina pastors and leaders live immersed in this reality. They need to understand what the community is experiencing, but they also need to reflect on the causes so that they can point toward solutions. The churches also need to recognize they do not stand outside of the complexities that have been described; they are an integral part of this reality. They play an important role in the community and will have an impact on any effort to address the problems mentioned. They will also play a role in defining the place of Latinos in US society. These are our people and here is where we are called to serve.

> Ministry in the Latino community in the United States needs to respond to the broad variety of needs in the community.
>
> PABLO ANABALÓN

2

Protestants and Latinos in the United States

The Latino experience in the United States presents a series of social and cultural complexities that complicate any pastoral ministry effort. Not only have we had different social, cultural, and historical experiences, we also have had varied religious experiences. In particular, the relationship between Latinos and US Protestants has contributed to that complexity of experiences.

Historical Review of Protestant Evangelization

Protestant churches from the United States began sending missionaries to Latin America during the first part of the nineteenth century. During that time, US Protestants also began to think about the "Mexicans" in what is now the Southwest part of the United States. After the conquest of 1848, several mission agencies spoke of the need to evangelize the conquered Mexicans, and some initial missionary efforts began during the 1850s. These produced the first converts and the first Latino Protestant churches. But it was not until after the Civil War (1861–65) that Protestants began working among the approximately 100,000 Mexicans that had stayed in the Southwest and become US citizens.

33

These initial contacts in the Southwest during the nineteenth century had a much smaller parallel among Cuban and Puerto Rican refugees, and Spanish and Latin American immigrants, in the eastern United States. But all of the Protestant missionaries had in common the link between evangelization and Americanization. They were sure that their task had to include the process of Americanizing the Latinos who now lived in the country. Many Protestant leaders were afraid that these Latinos, almost all Catholics, would hurt the country. In particular, they feared the possible influence of the Mexicans of the Southwest, because the Treaty of Guadalupe Hidalgo (1848), in which Mexico ceded the land of the Southwest after the US invasion of Mexico, also gave citizenship rights to those Mexicans who remained in the region.

> The most obvious challenges continue being false perceptions that generate socio-cultural, economic, and political realities that negatively affect the existence and quality of life of the Latino communities in the United States. These perceptions are both external and internal.
>
> OSCAR & KARLA GARCÍA

These initial mission efforts, and those that followed throughout the nineteenth and into the first part of the twentieth century, all worked from a deficiency perspective. Latinos were seen as people with many needs and the Protestants of majority culture had the responsibility to supply those needs. These people needed the gospel, but they also needed to learn US customs, the English language, hygiene, and technological advances. The Protestant missionaries and churches saw their mission among Latinos as their responsibility both as good Christians and as good US citizens.[1]

Throughout the twentieth and into the first years of the twenty-first century, there have been a series of waves of missionary interest and disinterest among Protestant groups toward Latino communities. Generally, interest has grown or declined depending on the migratory patterns of the period. As the number of *evangélicos* in Latin America has increased,

34

several denominations have expanded their ministries among Latinos in the United States, often using leaders imported from Latin America. Today, almost all Protestant denominations, be they conservative or liberal, have some ministry or church in the Latino community. Some have a long history in the community and others seemed to have recently discovered us. But interest in doing mission among Latinos seems to be growing.

Parallel to these efforts by majority-culture churches and denominations, Latino *evangélico* churches, mostly of Pentecostal background, have begun expanding their own ministries within the community. Many of these efforts have little relationship with traditional US denominations. Some of these movements were born in the US, while others have arrived with the new immigrants from Latin America. Much of the current growth of the Latino *evangélico* movement is happening in this type of church.

Relations between Latino and US Protestants

Protestant missionary work among Latinos has produced a number of growing churches and members. But these Latino churches have vary-

> It is a ministerial responsibility to know the history of the Latino church so that we can learn from our previous mistakes and also learn of many achievements we have had as Latinos in this country.
> SAÚL & ROSAMARÍA MALDONADO

ing types of relationships with majority culture Protestant churches.

Latino Churches in US Denominations

Protestant evangelization has produced many Latino converts whose relationship with US structures has not always been clear. The principal denominations that worked among Latinos during the nineteenth and the beginning of the twentieth century almost always formed the Spanish-language churches into separate districts or conferences. In the **35**

Southwest some of these districts were linked, formally or informally, with missionary efforts in Mexico. These organizations were not always very stable and some disappeared or were restructured as the status of Latino churches changed. Nonetheless, in some denominations these groupings were the basis for the growth and development of Latino leaders. In some of these denominations, Latino structures have been in existence for decades and a few are over a century old.

Other denominations or movements have begun "Latino ministries" more recently or have opted for hybrid models in which Latino churches are part of the same district or conference as all other churches but then have some parallel or informal structure so that Latino churches can relate and work together. To this day there are strong opinions on the value or limitations of having or not having Latino-specific structures within US denominations.

Some denominations have multiple structures for Latino churches. For example, the Assemblies of God has Latino districts, but also has Latino churches in "Anglo" districts and even a few Latino churches that are part of the Portuguese language district. This multiplicity of structures creates situations in which there are Latino churches of the same denomination ministering in the same community but having no direct denominational relationship between them.

These relations have become more complicated as the number of Latinos in "Anglo" churches continues to grow. Since the nineteenth century, many Latinos have become members of majority culture churches. Generally, it has been assumed that these people are more assimilated and that they do not want to express their Latino identity in church. The reality is that many of these Latinos continue to have strong Latino cultural ties but do not express them in church. Their culture and their religious experience express themselves in two very different spheres and many times these Latinos are "invisible" in majority culture churches.

Another recent phenomenon is the small, but growing, number of Latino pastors leading "Anglo" or multicultural congregations. These people are changing the traditional categories of ministry among different ethnicities and cultures and are forcing churches to think in new ways about what it means to minister in the Latino community.

Little by little, the number of Latino leaders in Protestant institutions is also growing. There are a growing number of Latinos in denominational structures, and in Protestant seminaries, universities, and schools. Some are there to minister to Latinos and do not have any major influence outside of the Latino community. Others seem to be in the opposite situation, where they have broad influence but they have very little space to directly support the Latino community. In some cases it is also not clear whether their function is basically to serve as tokens ("trophies") so that people can say that such and such organization "believes" in Latinos. Nonetheless, the number of Latinas in these types of institutions continues to grow and one can anticipate that their influence will also continue to grow.

Since the Latino community continues growing, many denominations, movements, and churches are waking up to the need and possibilities that ministry in the Latino community represents. Also, the denominations that have been working in the Latino community for many years are seeing the importance of increasing their missional commitment to the community. This means that intercultural relations in US denominations will continue becoming more complex as their demographic composition continues changing.

Latino and Latin American Denominations and Movements

On a parallel track to US denominational efforts are many completely Latino or Latin American movements and denominations that have established churches and ministries in the Latino community. Many of these efforts minister without any direct relationship to US denominations. Almost all of these movements have their origins in Pentecostalism or charismatic movements.

The first denominations of this type were born in the United States after the Pentecostal revival at the beginning of the **37** twentieth century. Others began in Latin America and were brought to the United States by immigrants. In the last part of the twentieth century, a proliferation of *evangélico* movements from Latin America or started by Latino pastors in the United States began appearing. Everything seems to indicate that the number of these new movements will continue to grow within the Latino community.

These movements have certain advantages in the Latino community. These structures are led by Latinos and are developing their own ministries. They create spaces to identify a new generation of leaders and can develop their own vision because they do not depend on outside leadership or on outside funds.

Nonetheless, these churches struggle with many of the same cultural complexities faced by other Latino Protestant churches. The movements started by US Latinos do not always understand the immigrants and vice versa. Immigrant church leaders many times attempt to continue their ministries the way they did them in their countries of origin and do not always understand the changes occurring among their members. Occasionally, they also struggle with the cultural and national mixes they experience here and with the cultural changes that their own children born and raised in the United States demonstrate.

These movements and churches are a clear reflection of the complexity of polycentric Latino identity. They have Latino leadership and are sustained by a Latino economic base. They provide a space for developing Latino leadership. Nonetheless, they cannot avoid many of the same cultural and social challenges confronted by Latino churches tied to US denominations.

Perspectives of Latino Ministry as Seen from US Churches and Denominations

US Protestant efforts among Latino communities tend to reflect certain patterns that are repeated by the different denominations. These illustrate the perspective that they have of the Latino community in relationship to the dominant society and the history the specific denomination has had among Latinos.

Ministry "to" or "for" Latinos

One of the most common models of Protestant ministry among Latinos is one in which Latinos are seen principally as objects of mission. This type of ministry begins when a church "discovers" the Latinos in their midst. Generally these projects seek to supply a perceived need among Latinos. If such a project has Latino leadership, that person is employed by the church or ministry and is supposed to follow that organization's direction. Some of these efforts provide significant services for the Latino community. But these efforts do not assume that Latinos will take responsibility for these efforts or that Latinos will be the principal people in charge of these projects.

> Generally the challenges [we face] as Latino leaders in the community are so large that we do not have sufficient resources and we need to approach and seek help from Anglo churches.
>
> MARÍA HAMILTON

Ministry "with" Latinos

Throughout the world one hears Christian organizations talking about the importance of forming partnerships between the "rich" world and the "majority" world. The goal in these efforts is for everyone to feel ownership of what is being done.

Many denominations and churches in the United States have developed, or seek to develop, this type of ministry model. Various denominations have strong Latino churches and leaders as part of their denominational structures. But, for the most part, their numbers are well below the percentage of Latino Protestants in the United States.

This type of model assumes that Latinos can take a certain level of responsibility for the project. When churches are established under this model, it is generally assumed that Latinos will take full responsibility for the leadership, vision, administration,

39

and finances of the church after a certain period of time, generally two to five years. The success or failure of these efforts many times depends on what is assumed that a church needs to have for an effective and self-sufficient ministry. When the goal is to produce a structure similar to that of majority culture churches, it is more difficult to establish a self-sustaining Latino church.

Latinos as Subjects of Mission

Parallel to these mission efforts, as previously mentioned, Latino churches with no direct links to US denominations have grown and thrived. The first of these efforts were born after the Azusa Street revival at the beginning of the twentieth century. Throughout the years, many movements, most of them small, have been born under Latino leadership and are sustained directly by Latinos.

Historically, Latinos who have migrated to the United States, be they Catholics or Protestants, have not "imported" their church and religious leaders, as did many European immigrants in previous generations. This has begun to change in the last decades. Many Latin American *evangélico* movements have established churches in the United States, mostly following the migratory patterns of their members. Most of these churches have few formal ties to US denominations and they maintain strong structural links to their home churches in Latin America.

Also, many Latino churches that have formal ties to US denominations direct and sustain their own ministries and projects. The number of Latino churches that do not depend on outside support continues to grow. These churches are beginning to change the perspective of dependence that had been assumed by many majority culture churches and denominations when thinking about ministry among Latinos.

Ministry among Latinos in Practice

Figure 2A charts out the "types" of ministry efforts of non-Latino congregations or ministries in the community and the growing place that Latinas can have in ministry in the community.

40

Figure 2A
*Models of ministry in the Latino community by majority
culture churches*

Ministries for the Community

Religious Services

Departments

Sister Congregations

Partnerships

Sister Churches

Independent or Interdependent

Growing Autonomy and Responsibility

Leadership — Vision — Program — Finances

Services for the community—Generally, US churches or denominations begin their commitment to the Latino community by offering a service or supplying a need. This type of response is common where Latinos are recent arrivals. Ministry tends to vary depending on the theological perspective of each church. Some of the more common efforts are English classes, tutoring for children, food for needy families, **41** support of day laborers, or job skills sessions. More conservative churches tend to offer more direct services, while more liberal churches often become involved in supporting Latinos as they deal with social or legal structures. In this model of ministry, Latinas are the recipients of the effort. It is assumed that because of their socioeconomic situation they have many needs and are not able to take responsibility in meeting them.

Religious services—It is common to see churches that have started some type of ministry among Latinos also include religious services in Spanish. In a sense this is another service for the community. Many times it is assumed that these services will be "temporary" and only for those who cannot participate in the English services, a type of ESL church. They might exist for many years, but they are always under the principal church and, generally, it is assumed that such religious services will never become independent churches. In fact, if the people participating in these services decided they wanted to organize themselves as a church, this may well spark opposition from majority culture church members.

Departments—Some churches take the next step and give the developing group some autonomy so that Latinos can develop under the direction of the larger church. These congregations have a level of autonomy in relationship to their internal work. Nonetheless, the "mother church" makes all key decisions, including issues of vision, mission, and budget. Some churches use this model as an intermediate step in the process of developing a new church. Others use it assuming that a self-sufficient Latino congregation will never develop given the particular circumstances of the community. Other churches may use this model persuaded that an independent Latino church should not develop.

Sister congregations—This type of model provides more autonomy even as it maintains organic ties between the new Latino congregation and the congregation that gave it life. Generally this means that the Latino congregation has a great deal of control over what it does. But it maintains structural connections, such as building usage, legal status, ministry and mission projects, or other types of links with the "mother"

42

church. This model of ministry is usually called a multi-congregational church.

Daughter churches—Also, some churches start ministries in the Latino community with the expectation that they will grow and will become responsible for their own ministry and leadership. In other cases, the project begins as religious services and begins to develop step by step until it reaches this final stage. In this perspective, the goal is to develop new churches that will be able to take full responsibility in relationship to their own future. When this model works, the result is a new church that can stand next to the "mother church" and be counted as another congregation in their denomination or movement.

Figure 2A illustrates that movement from left to right implies growing autonomy in leadership, finances, and vision. In some cases this might be an evolutionary process. But in others it has to do with the assumptions made about the Latino community and its place as object or subject of mission. The more Latinos are seen as a "needy" people, the more there is a tendency to minister toward the top left side of the diagram. The more the assumption is that Latinos should, or can, be subjects of their own mission project, the more that ministry is done toward the bottom right side.

Another important factor in this process has to do with the social and political vision that the ministering church has of the Latino community in the context in which it is doing mission. If the assumption is that the community is "transitory" and will soon assimilate and disappear as a distinctive community, or lose interest in having its own church, then the tendency is to do mission using models toward the top left of the diagram. The stronger the assumption that Latinos are a distinctive community with a distinctive future, the greater the tendency to seek to go toward the bottom right on this scale.

Ministry Tensions

As has been stated indirectly in previous sections, a very important issue in ministry among Latinos has to do with the social vision one has of Latinas in the United States. If one

43

assumes that Latinos are structurally assimilating, or should do so, then the tendency is to develop projects in which Latinos do not take a key role or will never develop distinctively "Latino" institutions. Many churches begin ministry among Latinos from the assumption that these never "should" be independent of the principal congregation.

This becomes more complicated when talking about "second" generations. Some ministries assume that Latino children will Americanize and so do not develop specific ministries for them. Instead they join them with the children of the principal church. The subconscious attitude seems to be that if they start a ministry in Spanish for the parents, "the children will be ours." In the model, the Latino church seemed to be limited to the ESL project, but extended by one generation.

This type of "temporary" mentality many times creates situations of dependence or codependence. Since no one expects the Latino congregation to become completely responsible for itself, a relationship of dependency develops. Latinos do not see the need to take responsibility and the principal congregation assumes that Latinos cannot become responsible. These mutual assumptions are mutually "verified," creating a situation of codependency in which each group sees the other as the cause of the "problem."

> The most difficult thing for me is the need to explain myself all the time. I am tired of having to explain and describe the way we work.
>
> DANNY MARTÍNEZ

This is complicated because of the differences among Latino groups. Many times a congregation with good intentions seeks out a Latino leader to minister in the community. But they do not always understand the differences in the community and they bring in a person who does not fit, does not know how to fit, or does not want to fit among the Latino subgroups in the community. Occasionally this person relates well to the principal congregation and is well received by them but finds it difficult to work in the specific Latino community. Those who began the ministry conclude that Latinos are not interested in supporting a church because they do not understand the intercultural issues among Latino subcultures.

44

The missional intentions of majority culture churches also become more complex because we Latinos do not have a common vision of the type of church or ministry we want to be a part of. A growing number of Latinos attend non-Latino churches; their reasons are quite varied. Some do it because they feel more comfortable in a majority culture context. Others because they want to connect to majority culture (marginal Latinos, assimilated Latinos, or those who are fleeing).

But there are also much more complex reasons. Some Latinas have a strong Latina identity in some areas of their lives, but not in the religious sphere. Others are convinced that majority culture "does church" better than Latinos, since they have more resources and more well-known pastors. From this perspective, the Latino church is only for those who cannot take advantage of the "best." Many others want to express their faith in an intentionally multicultural setting, one that reflects the way they live their lives. There is also the case of those Latinos who go to a majority culture church because it was through that congregation they found spiritual life. Our own differences and motivations are an indispensable part of the process of mission in the community. All this variety of Latino responses complicates the planning that a majority culture church or denomination might do when they want to work in the community.

Issues Raised by Protestant Ministry among Latinos

Protestant ministry in the Latino community calls us to ask questions about our identity, the relationship of *evangélicas* with other religious groups in the community, and the ways we understand our commitment to mission. Some of these questions do not have a clear answer. Nonetheless, they are issues that are part of the environment in which we minister.

Terms That Identify Us—"Evangélica" or "Evangelical" or "Protestant"

Latinos, and Latin American immigrants, often find ourselves between English and Spanish as we minister and even as we

45

identify ourselves. For many of us, *evangélico* has been a broad term that has included all or almost all Protestants. But many in the United States use *evangélico* as synonymous with evangelical. Since evangelical defines a specific movement in the United States, it is much more limited than the traditional use of *evangélico* in Spanish. Because of our particular histories here and in Latin America, the categories of majority culture churches in the United States do not always adequately describe Latino congregations. The question for us is whether our history or the history of majority Protestantism will define the terms that describe us. Can we continue being *evangélicas* in the Latino or Latin American sense that many of us have used the term, or will we have to adopt the categories of US Protestantism, Evangelical, Pentecostal, and mainline churches?[2]

Church, Culture, Language, and Identity

The issue of vocabulary leaves a more complex set of issues for those of us who are Protestant and Latino. What is a Latina *evangélica* or a Latino Protestant? Traditionally, Protestant churches have evangelized and Americanized Latinos, believing that both things were very important and, in a sense, even went together. To this date, many Protestant churches combine evangelization and Americanization, directly or indirectly, as they minister in the Latino community.

For many people, becoming a Protestant tends to be a sign of cultural assimilation. There are many Latinos who see becoming a Protestant as part of the process of cultural adaptation to this country. Therefore, some Latinos have no interest in an ethno-religious identity that is both Latino and Protestant.

On the other hand, Latino *evangélico* churches in the United States have played an important role in strengthening Latino culture and the Spanish language since the first Latino *evangélico* congregation was formed in the 1850s. Many Latinos born or raised in the United States learned to read and write in Spanish because of their participation in Latino churches. The church has been a key institution in the Latino cultural formation of several generations of Latinos. So Latino Protestant

46

churches are a part of identity formation for many Latinos. This challenges us to ask the question: what identity do we want, or should we want, to form?

Latino Evangélico Churches as Multicultural Realities

The person who observes Latinos from the outside often thinks that we are a monocultural group. But we already saw in the first chapter that the Latino community is in fact a series of communities. This means that most Latino churches are multicultural. They have people from different countries, people with different experiences in the United States, people with varied ethnic backgrounds and even different languages (not just Spanish or English). Any Latina pastor has to take this diversity into account if she wants to minister effectively.

This situation is complicated by the intercultural relations that exist in this country. We work alongside people from other minority groups and within majority culture. Our daughters and sons are marrying people of other cultures and ethnicities, and we are also sharing the good news of the gospel with people of various cultures. This means that our churches are becoming more multicultural every day. This creates both tension and opportunity for ministry in our communities.

Relations between Protestants and Catholics

One of the major issues in Latino Protestant ministry has to do with the relationship between Protestants and Catholics. Historically, the maj-

> Migration has provided a new field for the harvest that continues growing day by day. This requires the development of cultural competency that will give us a better understanding of the differences [among Latinos].
>
> JOSÉ GARCÍA

ority of *evangélicas* have had a Catholic background. The almost uniform testimony of those who left the Catholic Church is that they left because they did not find spiritual life in Catholicism. This perspective is even reflected in our hymnology.

47

Hay una senda[3]

Las amistades y tados mis parientes
Fueron las gentes que ya relacioné
Me aborrecieron por causa de su nombre
Cuando supieron que a Cristo me entrequé

Ya aquel camino de tantos sufrimientos
Aquel camino que el cielo me trazó
Fue transformado en aquel feliz momento
Cuando mi Cristo al cielo me llamó

For many Catholics, Protestant evangelization is seen as proselytism, though the great majority of those who joined Protestant churches are people who had a very marginal relationship with the Catholic Church. The tension in Latin America and in the Spanish-speaking world of the United States has been one in which Protestants have been a minority sometimes marginalized, and even persecuted, for their religious commitment. To this day the pope calls *evangélicos* in Latin America sects, a perspective shared by many of the bishops and cardinals of the continent.[4]

> The greatest challenge is how to work with Catholics without alienating them completely from their culture. We know that Latino culture has many influences from Catholicism, such as *posadas,* the Day of the Dead, and the Virgin of Guadalupe, things that at the same time are cultural. As Protestants or *evangélicos* we want recent converts to completely throw out their cultural-religious traditions, alienating them from the customs and their society (relations with the rest of the family not converted).
> FERNANDO SANTILLANA

Many Latin American immigrants arrive in the United States and see that, generally, the relationship between Catholics and Protestants is much more positive here than in Latin America; and this creates tension between them and the Protestant leaders in majority culture. These immigrants bring their experiences and their testimonies with them and they cannot understand why majority culture Protestant churches have positive relations with Catholics. Many also notice a difference between the practices of Latino Catholics and English-speaking Catholics.

Many of the historical tensions between Catholics and Protestants in Latin America are disappearing. But the theological differences continue. Also, the spiritual vitality of *evangélico* churches is attractive to many people with a Catholic background but who do not have significant ties to the Catholic Church. On the other hand, the complexities of our community make it indispensable that Catholics and Protestants work together to respond to the socioeconomic and political needs of our community. All this implies that we need to rethink the relationships between Latina *evangélicas* and Catholics.

Other Religious Expressions

Within the Latino community, there are also other religious groups. And since we live in the midst of a "shopping mall" of religious options, we can anticipate that some members of the Latino community will be drawn to other movements and religions. The religious movements that currently have the most influence can be divided into five major categories.

- First, there are those that come from our historical backgrounds. The religiosities of African or indigenous backgrounds continue having an impact as separate movements or as influences on the way many Latinos express their Christian faith.
- Second, there is both a Jewish and a Muslim presence among Latinos and Latin Americans. These communities are small, but some of them have a long history within our

49

Latino reality. Islam is also attracting a new generation of followers among Latinos in the United States.

- A third, very important, group, are movements like the Jehovah's Witnesses or the Mormons. They were born within Christianity, though they question some of the basic foundations of historical Christianity. These two groups have many followers among Latinos. There are also other similar groups in the community.
- A fourth category is that of Latinos who are joining other religious expressions, including world religions and new religions.
- A final category, and one that is growing, is that of secularized Latinos. Antireligious Latinos have always been part of the mix, but the growth of secularism is a fairly recent phenomenon in many parts of Latin America and among Latinos in the United States.

This religious diversity creates a pastoral environment that is more complex than what the Latino community had experienced in the past. Many times one finds this variety in one family. The challenge is to be able to respond to this growing religious diversity.

Life and Ministry on the Periphery

Many Latino churches are located on social peripheries. They are in poor barrios and in small agricultural communities. Very few Latino churches are located in areas of social or economic influence. Even the few that are in middle class neighborhoods often have a precarious financial base. Tied to this is the fact that many Latino immigrants are in a precarious legal situation.

> Latinos know and have experienced migration, poverty, and discrimination. Our community needs to respond to our own experience by being an administrator of God's love for the poor and those who cannot fend for themselves.
>
> DANNY MARTÍNEZ

The reality of poverty and the unsure legal situation of many in the Latino community mean that we need to find creative ways to minister with limited resources. Ministry on the periphery means opening spaces and hope to people who many times are struggling to survive. Nonetheless, this demands a leadership that understands Latino realities and that can respond in such circumstances. It also means a commitment to serve in the midst of poverty and difficulty.

> God has chosen the Latino community in these last days to evangelize the world. Proof of this is the growth of the Latino church in the United States and throughout Latin America.
>
> SERGIO NAVARRETE

Latinos as Agents of Mission in the United States and the World

The tentative reality of many Latinas and Latinos seems to open up spaces and opportunities for mission. Growing numbers of immigrants are taking their faith to each place where they move. They are not missionaries in any formal or traditional sense. But they are people with a clear sense of mission. Wherever they go they see themselves as people that God can use to share the good news of the gospel. Since they do not have positions of power and do not come from powerful countries, they are not seen as a threat or as representatives of a culture that wants to impose itself on others. Their movement presents a unique opportunity for ministry that is yet to be fully drawn upon.

This same spirit can be seen in a growing number of Latino churches. As the number of Latino churches continues growing, a missionary vision among US Latinos continues expanding. This growing commitment is changing the historically dependent relationship between Latino and majority culture churches.

3

Resources within the Latino Community and Church

Historically, ministry in the Latino community has been motivated or oriented by deficiency models. Ministries have been defined around the needs of the Latino community and how to respond to them. In the nineteenth century Protestant missionaries were sure that the conquered Mexicans would not be able to participate in US society unless the missionaries Americanized them. Many people in the US agreed with a type of social Darwinism that doubted whether there was any point in attempting to incorporate people, like the Mexicans, who were not "pure race" Europeans to US citizenship.

Today one can hear churches or leaders say that it does not make sense to work with immigrants or that ministry among them should basically consist of cultural adaptation processes. The solution proposed by this perspective is that the future of Latinos depends on letting go of their "Latino-ness" as soon as possible. This perspective is also seen in educational efforts that encourage Latino youth to disassociate themselves from their family and customs to "succeed" in US society.[1]

This type of perspective tends to focus on the deficiencies of the community and concludes that the future of the Latino community, if there is one, is to assimilate as soon as possible and to lose their particular identity. Distinctive Latino culture is a burden that is limiting the Latinos' future and that can potentially harm US society.

It is crucial to respond to the needs of the community, but this process easily degenerates into one in which Latinos are only the object of mission without taking into account the resources and strengths that the Latino community brings to pastoral work. We want to address this tendency by focusing on what the Latino community offers to ministry among Latinas and beyond.

Where We Are Today

The Pew Research Center has funded several important studies of Latinos and in particular our religious tendencies. Two of the most important studies in the religious arena, *"Hispanic Churches in American Public Life"* (2003) and *"Changing Faiths—Latinos and the Transformation of American Religion"* (2007) describe us as a community with strong religious identifications and a strong religious identity linked to Latino identity.[2]

Both the 2003 and 2007 studies described similar religious preferences within the Latino community. According to the second study, 67.6 percent of Latinos are Catholic and 19.6 percent are Protestants. Other Christian groups like the Mormons and Jehovah's Witnesses constitute 2.7 percent of the population, while secular people or those who do not identify with any particular Christian group make up 7.8 percent. The numbers are similar to the 2003 study, though they do not match exactly, in part because the questions used in the two studies were not exactly the same.

According to the 2007 study:

• Latinos will be a growing percentage of the Catholic Church. More than a third of Catholics in the United States today are Latinos and that percentage will continue growing.

- There is a generational tendency toward becoming Protestant. The percentage of Latino Protestants is higher among those who have been in the United States three or four generations than among immigrants.
- Clearly marked religious differences exist among the different Latino groups. For example, people with a Mexican background tend to be more Catholic (74 percent), while less than half of Puerto Ricans identify themselves as Catholics (49 percent) and 14 percent of those of Cuban background identify themselves as secular.
- There seems to be a relationship between religious identity and ethnic identity within the Latino community. According to the study, the vast majority of Latinos go to churches that have three key characteristics: they have Latino pastors or priests, they offer services in Spanish, and they have a Latino majority in the congregation. This tendency seems to be important not only for immigrants, but also among US-born Latinas.

Other studies also are analyzing various aspects of Latino religiosity. In particular, new studies are examining the differences between Latino religious expressions and those of majority culture in the US. The Pew-funded studies analyzed Latinos through the lenses of US religiosity. Several important differences between Latinos and majority culture have implications that have not yet been clarified:

- Many Latino Catholics have a strong popular religious devotion. But this commitment cannot be necessarily measured by their participation in the official services of the Catholic Church. There are very committed Latino Catholics who do not participate very much in the formal structures of the Catholic Church.
- Other expressions of popular religiosity, such as those of Afro-Caribbean or indigenous background, can be found in the Latino community. Many of these expressions cross religious lines and are practiced even by people who call themselves secular.

55

- The Latino religious experience includes Latin American and US elements. US religious categories do not always match Latino experiences. For example, as previously stated, many Latino Protestants use the term *evangélico* in Spanish in a way not synonymous with evangelical in English.[3] On the Catholic side, it is important to recognize that the Latino Catholic charismatic movement has Latin American and Spanish influences. It is not completely the same as US charismatic movements.
- The Latino community contains a great deal of religious movement and multiple religious options. There are people with multiple and changing religious identities who cannot easily be defined using exclusive religious categories.

The Pew studies and the growing number of analyses of Latino religiosity also indicate that Latinos are not merely objects of mission, but that they are transforming the religious direction of the United States. The Latino community is a growing community with strong religious tendencies that is becoming an agent of its own religious future. This community has many resources for responding to the challenges it has before it.

Tools and Resources Latinos Bring to Ministry

As we think about ministering in the Latino community, we need to take into account the needs we have already mentioned. But US Latino cultures have many assets on which churches can draw when it comes time to respond to the needs of the community. Before we begin to describe models and types of ministry, which we will do in the next chapter, we want to describe some of the advantages that the community has as it responds to its own needs.

A Live Faith in God

As previously stated, several important studies have demonstrated the strong religiosity of the Latino community.[4] Clearly, the vast majority of Latinos believe in God as someone who participates in daily life. We are a people of strong religious devotion that manifests itself in daily life (*lo cotidiano*) through devotion, prayer, participation in Bible studies, and in being an active part of churches. That faith in God is part of the frame that defines Latino culture. It is extremely difficult to describe the Latino community without taking into account its profound faith, religious devotion, and its expectation that God is part of human reality. All of this reflects a worldview in which God and the presence of spiritual beings are part of the human experience.

Believing in the active presence of God in human reality creates an environment of hope in the midst of very difficult circumstances. This hope makes it possible to develop support services and unite the community

> For me the most positive part of working in the Latino community is the enthusiasm that I find. Our people tend to have a great deal of enthusiasm, no matter how difficult life has been. Immigrants, in particular, have great courage. Otherwise, they would not have confronted the dangers of getting here.
>
> LUIS HERNÁNDEZ

to address specific needs. There is a willingness to make sacrifices to respond to complex problems because there is a faith in the presence of God by our side. This sense of sacrifice and hope makes it possible to continue when the process is slow and one does not see immediate results.

It is also possible to appeal to common religious experiences, or common religious perspectives, when serving in the community. We have a variety of religious experiences, but most of us share a common religious worldview and spirituality. This perspective is very different from the more rational religiosity common in many Western countries. God is not a doctrinal concept, but a relationship and an experience in daily life. This experience is lived alongside others in the life of the church or in popular devotion.

This faith in God shows itself in the way many Latino Protestants read the Bible. The Bible speaks to us and calls us **57** to listen to God. This devotional and pre-critical reading invites us to read the Latino experience in light of the divine presence. In the midst of poverty and marginalization, one finds the God that offers me the opportunity to be a person of value, God's child, in the power of the Holy Spirit.[5]

To believe in God is also to approach God in worship from the depth of being. *Evangélica* worship is participatory, passionate, and multicultural, a fiesta where people celebrate God. This worship can occur in homes or in simple places of worship, because there is a clear sense of God's presence anywhere God's people come together.

Ministry Where People Are

The great majority of Latino churches are located where the people live. The small urban churches that rent facilities in poor barrios and the rural Latino churches are immersed in the complexity of the people. These churches are already ministering on the margins and the peripheries of US society. This is where much of the Latino community is, and it is here that ministry is needed in order to have a long-term impact.

Many leaders and congregations do not have strong and clearly defined concepts of social justice, nor adequate tools to analyze and respond to the needs of the community. But they do have clarity about the needs of the people and know that they need to respond. These congregations are ministering to the real needs of the community because they are the same needs as those of the members of the churches or of their relatives, friends, or neighbors. It is in the midst of these needs that people read the Bible and discover God's love that responds to their situation. It is here people discover that God walks with them in the midst of pain and difficulty.[6]

It is on the periphery where poor Latino churches practice mutual aid and commitment toward the needy and discarded of society. Here God's love is shown through concrete actions by real people. These churches provide space and leadership for people marginalized and forgotten by a society that measures success by criteria that these people will likely never reach.

These churches are also a challenge to the church in the majority society and to Latinos who have achieved their "American dream." They call us to recognize that we cannot help the needy if we do not identify with them and if we do not live where they live. To the extent that we can leave the centers of power and

> My desire is to see Christians relocate into urban areas wherever we have departed from the needy—especially Hispanic and African-American communities. On the other hand, I would like to see those Christians already living in these areas stay put, as difficult as that may seem. It is Christ who sustains us and maintains our destiny. The church that was located in the city but has migrated to better surroundings may need to review its vows toward the community and the poor.
>
> MANUEL ORTIZ
> HISPANIC CHALLENGE[7]

go to where Latino churches are, we will be able to demonstrate God's love. Latino churches are already located where all of us who want to serve the poor and needy need to be.

Flexible Cultural Models

The majority of Latino cultures have lived in the midst of *mestizajes* [cultural, ethnic, or racial mixes] for centuries. The Spaniards imposed a *mestizaje* on the indigenous peoples and the slaves from Africa, though the pre-Colombian peoples had already experienced various types of *mestizajes*, voluntary or forced. New migrations into the Spanish-speaking world have expanded the cultural influences on Latino communities. Even though there is an amount of cultural and racial "purity" among the upper classes and a great deal of racism against the native peoples and those of African descent, the majority of Latinos in this country are *mestizos* or mulattoes. We know that we were born and have been formed in the midst of many cultures and ethnicities. Some of us are tempted to appeal to some racial "purity," but the vast majority of us know that we are daughters and sons of multiple encounters between different peoples and ethnicities.

59

> God works untiringly to reconcile and renovate the cultural spaces that destroy and oppress God's creation. The culture in which we were born is a divine gift and an acquired culture is an opportunity to enrich and develop ourselves without rejecting what we inherited.
>
> OSCAR & KARLA GARCÍA

This cultural mixing is reflected in the flexibility and cultural adaptation in the community. The encounters among various Latino peoples here in the United States have created new *mestizajes*, but they also have required the use of cultural flexibility. Latino churches in almost all urban centers and in many rural areas are multicultural. Our *mestizaje* experiences have been indispensable as we experience new cultural encounters, even within the Latino community. The average Latino church includes people of several Latin American countries, people born in the United States, someone from a minority group from Latin America, and some non-Latinos who have married someone from the congregation.

This cultural flexibility is also a very useful tool as we encounter people from many other cultures. The challenges of intercultural relations are eased because we already have experiences and patterns of relationships with people of other cultures. We confront racial and ethnic tensions in this country, but we can also count on these intercultural tools to create new types of bridges between the various peoples of the United States.

These mixes have also given us a framework for reflecting on our relationship with God and God's moving in our world. Our experiences as *mestizos* give us other ways to read the Bible and to perceive God's work in the world.[8] Because we cannot claim a racial "purity," we realize that our dignity comes from being sons and daughters of God and not because of some human merit or privilege. This opens the door for us to minister with more freedom among other peoples in our midst.

The Latina experience and our encounters in the United States give us assets particularly necessary for the church in this country. We urgently need models of intercultural church life in which uniformity is not imposed, but rather in which diversity is celebrated in the midst of unity. Since we are a group that already lives in intercultural relations, but from below, we have the possibility of offering new models of what it means to celebrate unity and diversity in the life of the US church.

Willingness to Work Arduously

The Latino community is contributing a great deal to the US economy. Our people are performing the most difficult and arduous tasks in the national economy. It is Latinos who work in the fields; who build our homes; who clean our offices, our hotels, and the homes of the rich; and who cook and clean in our restaurants. The Latino contribution to the national economy continues to grow.[9]

The majority of Latinas work assiduously, hoping to be able to improve their economic situation and to be able to help their families here and in their countries of origin, if they are immigrants. They dream of a better future and are making great sacrifices to make that dream a reality. Even the economic sacrifices and physical dangers faced by the undocumented that come to this country are a reflection of a disposition to do everything possible to improve their lot, no matter how difficult it may be.

This same disposition is seen in many Latino *evangélico* churches. Many of the congregations have a limited economic base. But they go forward because they have people willing to make this same type of sacrifice for the churches where they have found life and support. One also finds many bi-vocational pastors in the community. Many of these people make great sacrifices because they believe in what they are doing and that God will bless their sacrifice. This type of disposition makes it possible to establish and maintain Latino congregations among people with few economic or educational resources.

61

As previously mentioned, this disposition tends to be strongest among churches and movements that have limited ties to US denominations. The opportunity to take responsibility opens the space for people to become the subjects of their own ecclesial commitments.

Family and Community

Traditionally, the Latino concept of family has been broader than the nuclear family that serves as the common definition of family in the US. Family includes grandparents, uncles and aunts, cousins, and nieces and nephews. It also includes those who have become a part of the family by marriage. But the concept is often broader than that and includes people whose relationship to the family cannot be "exactly" defined. For many people it also includes those who are from "my hometown" or "*mi colonia.*" All of these people are part of "the family."

Family becomes more important because it defines part of a more collective identity within the community. As a member of this family, I have a responsibility toward all its members, including those with whom there is not a good relationship. I can also count on the support of family, even when the situation is difficult.

One of the most important motivations for migration to the United States is family. Some come to improve the economic situation of their families in their countries of origin. Others bring their families because they dream something better for their children. When they arrive in this country, they seek out relatives, knowing that they will help them somehow, even if with a bad attitude.

The Latino family has been the basis for socioeconomic support in difficult situations. Even in the midst of poverty, many families have been able to maintain a level of mutual care because they have been willing to help each other. There is a multitude of examples of poor families that live "better" than their income would seem to indicate because of the mutual support the extended family provides.

Of course, one needs to avoid the danger of idealizing the Latino family. Machismo and domestic violence are realities among Latinos, and the church has to confront these evils. We cannot continue covering up these problems in the name of family "well-being."

Nonetheless, the family has provided a great deal of support in the midst of poverty and need. Many people have seen themselves supported by their families and have been able to go forward because they have a base of security in the family. Even in the midst of the family disintegration that one sometimes sees in the Latino community, there is still this concept a family that can help in ministering in the community.

Latino churches can strengthen the social ties in Latino communities by supporting the family and appealing to the traditional Latino concept of family. US society tends to push toward individualism, where the commitment to family is sometimes seen as a burden. Nonetheless, our young people

> God loves everyone but I see that the Latino community has very deep roots in relationship to family and we can be an example in the church of what it means to be the family of God, demonstrating and teaching what it means to be parents and children. It is part of our DNA and I believe that as part of our DNA we can be a tremendous model to the church in general.
>
> ADELITA GARZA

and the weak in our community need the support of the extended family (as do also those who are sure they can function well without having family nearby). The Latino family offers the opportunity of providing roots and identity to young people, a container in which they can develop to then spread their wings as they participate in US society.

We urgently need to translate the Latino concept of family to postmodern US reality to take advantage of the Latino cultural reality. This traditional concept has much to offer a society that is in the midst of change and insecurity.

Some biblical images that tie together well with the ideal Latino family are church as the family of God and as community. **63**

In the midst of rapid social changes and the sense of dislocation caused by migration and movement, the church as family and community can provide support and care to people who are far from their blood relatives. The majority of Latino churches are fairly small. But this size makes it easier to draw on the New Testament model of a house-church for the Latino community today.

We could mention other strengths that come from our particular cultural experiences. These have allowed us to continue and prosper in the midst of adverse situations throughout the centuries. As we approach ministry in the Latina community, it is indispensable that we appeal to these images. This will keep us from focusing on the deficiencies. As we change our perspective, Latinos and Latinas will be subjects in God's mission in the Latino community and beyond.

4

What Latino Churches Are Doing

Latino *evangélico* churches are growing. There are no exact figures, but all types of Latino Protestant churches report growth, though the fastest growth is seen in Pentecostal or charismatic churches. The number of Latinas attending non-specifically Latino churches is also growing. The increasing diversity of the community is challenging churches to continue broadening their concepts and styles of ministry. Everything seems to indicate that Latino churches will continue growing, but also that they will need to continue diversifying to continue responding to the complexity represented by the Latino community.

Diversity and Its Growing Implications

In the first chapter we presented a diagram (figure 1A) to explain the differences among Latinas in relationship to identification with Latino culture and with majority culture in the United States. If we take this diagram into account and consider the types of Protestant churches currently serving in the community, we can divide ministry in the Latino community into three broad categories. These are not exclusive or black and white. But they do generally reflect the types of churches and ministries that are working among Latinas.

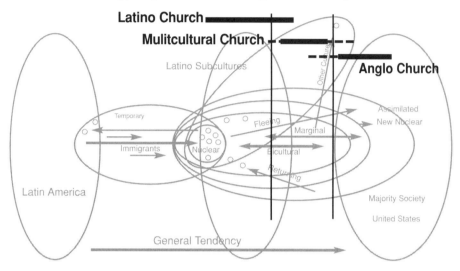

Figure 4A

Types of ministries among Latinos today

Churches with a clear Latino focus are ministering most successfully among people who have a strong cultural identification with the Latino community. This type of church has a very good ministry among people who live in barrios or in communities with a high Latino concentration. The majority of these types of churches minister among people who speak Spanish, though one can also find these types of churches ministering in English, or in variant forms of Spanglish, such as Tex-Mex. They are also able to minister effectively among bicultural Latinas or people who are returning to their Latino roots. Another group that can often be found in these churches is Latinos who grew up in Latino *evangélico* churches and who appreciate a service in Spanish or with a Latino "flavor," even though they live other aspects of their lives the same as majority culture. As probably seems obvious, a church that identifies itself as Latina will generally have very little impact among people who have limited identification with Latino culture.

At the other extreme we find churches clearly identified with majority culture. They are attracting Latinas assimilated into majority culture, marginal Latinos, and people who are fleeing from Latino culture. Some Latinos are also being attracted to mega-churches with a majority culture flavor the same as many other people in the United States. What is often attractive is the pastor or the ministry. Generally, Latinos play a minimal role in these types of churches. A church with strong majority culture identification is generally not attractive to people with a strong Latino cultural identity.

Between these two "extremes" of the nuclear Latino and the assimilated Latino lies a large percentage of the Latino community that has some type of bicultural or polycentric identity. Many of these people seek to celebrate the diversity that they live day to day. Though the number of churches that are intentionally multicultural is relatively small, congregations of this type are having an impact among this type of Latina. Some of these churches are multicultural within the diversity of the Spanish-speaking world, but the vast majority are ministering to the broader multicultural diversity of the United States.

The vast majority of churches minister within one of these mega-categories. But a growing number of churches are developing a variety of ministries to respond to this variety of cultural realities. Within the Latino community one sees growing numbers of congregations that are intentionally serving within the Latino community, while they are also developing a ministry that includes people of other ethnic backgrounds. They are attempting to minister within this diversity and at the same time work toward a multicultural and multiethnic unity that does not push toward uniformity.

This diagram reinforces what we have said in other parts of the book. There is not one Latino community, culturally speaking, nor only one Latino experience that defines all US Latinas. Whoever ministers in the Latino community will need to understand this great variety of cultural and social experiences that Latinos represent. And since these differences exist in the same Latino family, one cannot flee from, nor ignore, this reality.[1]

This diagram also illustrates three important realities when ministering in the Latino community.

67

- In the first place, one can anticipate that the Latino community will continue diversifying as it continues growing. Latinos, be they born in this country, or the immigrants who will continue arriving, are responding in different ways to our participation in US society; and this diversity will become more pronounced as the community continues growing.
- Second, the growth of the Latino community implies that there will be a need to continue establishing new churches and ministries with a Latino focus to respond to the growing Latino population.
- The third reality is that it will be necessary to develop new models of service and ministry that take into account the polycentric reality of a large percentage of the Latino community.

Just as there is not one single cultural definition that applies to all Latinos, there will also not be one single type of ministry that will be able to have an impact among the diverse Latino population.

The Pew study cited in the previous chapter (*Changing Faiths: Latinos and the Transformation of American Religion*) seems to indicate that the vast majority of Latinos who participate in churches prefer to be in congregations that have three characteristics: services in Spanish, Latina pastors, and a strong Latino presence among its members. This tendency is much stronger among Latinos who live in areas with a large Latino population concentration. But this phenomenon was also observed among Latinos where the population concentration is low, among third- and fourth-generation Latinos, and among Latinos who speak English as their principal (or only) language. This seems to indicate that the majority of Latinos who go to church want to participate in an environment where Latino culture is taken seriously in one way or another.

Since the Latino community is a polycentric community in movement, this situation might change in the future. But at this moment it is clear that a growing number of Latino churches or churches with a strong Latino focus are necessary. This implies continuing with the types of ministries that are already being done, but also the need of developing new models of ministry in the community, models that take into account the importance of the churches as missional entities that develop in concrete cultural contexts.

Latino Churches in the Community

Since the first Latino *evangélico* congregation was established in New Mexico in the 1850s, the number of Latino churches in the United States has been growing. New churches continue being established, and the new wave of Latino migration throughout the United States has taken new Latino *evangélico* churches to parts of the country where they had not been seen before. One also sees new churches in areas where the Latino community has existed for many years. For example, southern California has thousands of Latino churches and the number continues to grow.

In almost all US denominations and in every corner of the country, you will find Latina churches. The majority of the Latino churches are small, with fewer than one hundred active adult members. But there are also Latino churches in the principal urban centers of the country with thousands of members. As stated earlier, the churches that are growing the most are Pentecostal or those that have been "Pentecostalized." United States–based denominations are starting new Latino churches, but the number of Latino churches that are part of Latino and Latin American denominations or movements are also growing, as are independent churches.

Latino *evangélico* churches are very different among themselves, reflecting the

When more prosperous times come to some members of the congregation, they tend to move to "greener" areas, leaving voids in the leadership and economic support of the congregation. Those that minister in transitional neighborhoods generally resign themselves to the reality of having churches in flux and they find themselves with the embarrassing task of having to explain to the diocese, year after year, why their membership is not stable and how this affects the self-sufficiency of the parish.

SOFÍA HERRERA

69

multiple differences in the Latina community. But there are also certain characteristics that tend to be similar among the vast majority of these churches. These are related to the people to whom they minister, the places where they serve, the leadership of the churches, the atmosphere in which they live, and the religiosity that is practiced.

Churches on the Move

Latino *evangélico* churches reflect their members and the people among whom they serve. Latinos in the United States are a people on the move. Many Latinas arrived as immigrants from another country, but there are also many Latinos who continue to move around the country. Both Latinos born in this country and those who recently arrived are on the move, looking for better work opportunities, housing, or education. Latino young people also move, looking to open up new opportunities. Many churches have to develop their programs and projects around the premise that their people will leave after a while and that new people will take their place.

Many Latino churches feel as tentative as their members. They rent meeting spaces in the middle of urban areas. They use the buildings of other churches when these are not using them. Some have to move each time the building owner wants to raise the rent or the church that has rented them facilities decides to change its ministry focus. Nonetheless, these churches are where the Latino community lives. They live the sojourner and exile experience of the community. They are on the move because this is the reality of the people.

We have the vision of psychologically and spiritually lifting up the community, in the home, in their neighborhood or barrio, and in their place of employment. We want to raise them to a level where they understand that one has been placed here by God as a leader.

JIM TOLLE

But this movement is also serving as the impetus for the establishment of Latino churches around the country. Anywhere that Latinos settle, there are also believers that attempt to establish a congregation. There are also denominations and ministries in these places ready to support them in this task. So this movement opens new opportunities for ministry even as it makes it more difficult to strengthen existing ministries.

Marginal Churches

The vast majority of Latino churches are in barrios, predominantly Latino communities, and marginal farming areas. Since many Latinos live in marginal areas, it is not surprising that the congregations are here.

These congregations also reflect the marginality of the Latino community in many ways. The majority of their members tend to be people marginalized by society. They perform jobs with little prestige and many times are in "invisible" positions. Their labor is indispensable, but their presence is questioned, particularly if they are undocumented or if the broader community perceives them to be undocumented. Generally they have less formal education than the majority population, and the schools in the areas where they live usually have many deficiencies. Many of these communities also have deficient social services.

This perception of marginality is also seen in the denominations of which these churches are a part. They are generally perceived as small and weak, dependent on the denominational structure, without being able to make a significant contribution to the life of the churches.

But people in need are in the margins and it is from there that they can be lifted. Many Latino churches are places where marginalized people find hope and a space to develop. They receive divine power to rise out of destructive situations. But they also have the opportunity to develop as people. They can be leaders in churches even though they may not be given many

> Our response to the needs of the Latino community is focused on using all the resources we can to help those less favored [in society].
> LUIS HERNÁNDEZ

71

opportunities in other contexts. They learn that before God they are people of value, even when others despise them. The Latino church is also a place where people find help and support, the needy among the needy willing to help each other.

Community Churches

We have already mentioned the concept of the Latino church as family or community, and we will say more about this in the last chapter. At this point we want to mention that these churches tend to want to be an alternative community in which there is mutual commitment, one for the other. In the small Latino churches, all are a part and all are necessary. Many churches do not have a full-time pastoral ministry. The leaders are bi-vocational people who minister from a profound commitment, serving among the people with whom they live and work. Since many Latino churches are small, not only is there room for all, everyone is needed.

These churches are also part of the community in the sense that they attract people from around the church and respond to the need of their immediate community. They are in the midst of the needs of their people and minister to these needs.

Missional Churches

The majority of these community churches have a strong missionary impulse. God has become present in the lives of the members and they want to invite others to also enjoy that presence. People who have had destructive habits or destroyed lives experience the marvelous work of God in their lives and they want others to receive the

The Latino community finds the resurrected Christ in the Latino church. We also dare to say that the Latino church finds "the crucified Christ, disfigured by sin and oppression" in the Latino community. God's mission, then, occurs in the act of "accompaniment, reconciliation, and renewal" of the Latino church within the Latino community.

OSCAR & KARLA GARCÍA

same gift. Their personal experience of conversion creates an enthusiasm and serves as a motivation for fulfilling the divine mission. This disposition becomes indispensable for communities in constant movement, since they need to attract new members to replace the people who move to new locations. The people in movement from other places become part of new congregations or they serve as the core for beginning new Latino churches in those new places to which Latinas are moving.

Churches with Latina Leaders

Latino *evangélico* churches represent one of the few spaces where Latinos and Latinas have been able to be at the forefront of their own organizations in this country for more than a century. Almost all Latino churches have Latino pastors and leaders. The pastors that are not Latinos have a strong commitment to the Latino community and are training Latinas to assume leadership in these congregations.

This training is a key factor in the Latino community. Their church is where Latinas who have a limited voice in other contexts can develop leadership and raise up a new generation of leaders. Many Latino leaders have found their voice and their first opportunities for leadership in the Latino church. Since this is a place where everyone understands the cultural rules for decision making, it allows for the participation of people for whom it would be difficult to find their voice in another congregation. But it has also been a space for the Latino community to reflect on its own future and where the future is not determined by non-Latino leaders.

Churches with a Latino Spirit

An important component in the vast majority of Latino churches is the liberty to worship God through Latino culture. Since these are multicultural churches in the midst of US reality, these churches reflect the *mestizaje* of their members. They recognize that they can approach God through their Latino reality lived out in the United States. The services in these

73

churches reflect *Latinidad*, but also the reality of being Latino in this country.

This Latino focus provides the immigrant a place where she can feel safe, providing a link to the experiences from her country of origin. It also provides a space for those born in this country to develop and maintain Latino cultural and religious customs. The churches reflect the multiple *mestizajes* lived out by Latinas in the United States and are one of the few places where they can express their faith in God in a way that affirms their Latino identity.

Churches Where God Is Present

The worldview of the majority of Latinos is one in which God is present in the midst of life. One worships God because God has worked in concrete situations. The people pray for their needs to be met because they know that God works on behalf of a people who seek God. The testimonies of the members recognize that God has accompanied them and has worked on their behalf in situations that did not seem to have a solution. The believers read the Bible, participate in Bible studies, and listen to sermons in anticipation of hearing the word of God for their lives. At their best, these sermons are messages of hope, calling people to believe that God is concerned about them and inviting them to trust in God's future. This enthusiasm makes it possible for Latino churches to thrive in very adverse situations. The congregation knows that God is present; therefore, the members go forward even if it takes a great deal of sacrifice.

Models of Ministry That Have Developed in the Midst of Social Changes

The demographic changes that are occurring in many parts of the country have forced us to consider new ways of doing ministry in the Latino community. During the last few years, new ministry models have developed that reflect both the

74

diversification of the Latino community and also the changes occurring in majority culture churches.

Since the nineteenth century, Latinos have become members of majority culture churches. There are many reasons for this participation. Some congregations in historical (mainline) denominations have had Latino members for several generations. This type of church usually has Latino members without a specific ministry focus to include them. Their numbers are usually relatively small in this type of congregation. But it is important to recognize that some Latinos will be more attracted to majority culture churches than to churches with a Latino focus.

Nonetheless, changing cultural realities in the United States have created other models of church. Some of these have been in existence for over a generation, though they tend to be relatively new for the majority of churches and denominations. These models have begun growing, though they represent a limited number of churches working within Latino reality.[2]

Multiple Churches Working Together

One of the models that reflects the changing cultural environment is the decision of several churches of different cultural backgrounds to work together. It might be one church renting to another or several churches of the same denomination sharing a building. Each congregation has its own distinct leadership, is responsible for its own commitments, and has a specific mission. They celebrate their unity principally by joint usage of resources to advance their ministries. They may share a service or other activity together, but their congregational lives are almost completely independent of each other.

Sometimes this model begins for very pragmatic reasons. One congregation needs a place to meet and another one needs to generate extra income because it cannot fully deal with its economic commitments. Some majority culture congregations use this model in the hope that this type of arrangement will open doors for them to minister among the children of the Latino congregation.

75

But many other congregations that want to be a blessing to other ethnic groups use this method to support the ministry of others, particularly congregations from their own denomination or tradition. This model has been used in many places to start new Latino churches or to support projects that need external help. It has also served in many occasions as the first step toward a relationship that continues growing as the two congregations get to know each other better. It is likely that this ministry model will continue being the first contact point between many congregations given the costs of buying or renting a building in many urban centers.

Multi-congregational Churches

Multi-congregational churches are sister congregations, each of which has its own cultural, social, or linguistic focus. They share facilities and coordinate their ministries at some level. Some also share budgets. This model has become popular in urban centers and serves as a reflection of the cultural mixes and encounters of the city.

There are several types of multi-congregation churches:

- In the first type, the majority culture congregation (or the founding congregation if a different cultural group began the ministry) is the principal church and the others are "daughters." The principal congregation tends to be the "orchestra" leader and makes the primary decisions.
- In a second type of multi-congregational church, there is more equality among the congregations. Generally, this model develops in situations where none of the congregations is stronger than the others. It might be that the majority culture congregation owns the building, but it is not very strong, or it might even be in a process of decline.
- Another model, much less common, is one in which a minority group is the principal congregation and it opens its ministry location to other minority groups.
- Even less common is the model where various minority congregations work together, taking advantage of

facilities and of resources, without any majority culture representation.

The leadership of these congregations varies from those that have a single leadership team to those that have separate leadership for each congregation and have a coordinating group to direct joint efforts. These congregations have some activities together to celebrate their unity, but they each also maintain a level of autonomy to develop separate ministries and mission. Generally, each congregation has its own pastor, though there are situations in which one pastor leads more than one congregation.

This model provides the opportunity to share resources and to celebrate the unity of the church, while it gives groups the autonomy to develop ministries within their specific communities. It also allows the development of ministry in various languages, without imposing English on all of the groups. One of the principal challenges of this model is the coordination among the groups, particularly if one of them has access to many more resources than the other groups, something that is common when a majority culture church opens itself up to this type of ministry with ethnic groups that have fewer economic resources.

This model offers the opportunity of celebrating both the unity and the diversity of the church. Each group engages in separate activities that permit and celebrate diversity, while they also do things together, which allows them to confess the unity of the church in concrete ways.

Multicultural Churches

In the last few years, the number of intentionally multicultural churches in the United States has grown. These congregations seek to be faithful to the biblical vision of the church as a multicultural community by attracting people of different ethnicities and cultures into a single congregation. The vast majority of these congregations have their worship services in

English, though there are intentionally multicultural churches that use other languages, particularly Spanish.

Multicultural churches often attract people from different cultural backgrounds who have other things in common. What one sees in many congregations is not a common ethnic or cultural identity but rather socioeconomic or educational similarity. These churches celebrate their cultural diversity in the use of artifacts like music or food. Generally, their structure and organization reflect majority culture.

Some multicultural churches are struggling to bring together people with cultural and socioeconomic differences. This type of church attempts to bring together marked ethnic differences without imposing a dominant culture. They seek to celebrate and reflect the diversity of their community. These congregations struggle to maintain a balance in which each ethnic or cultural group can feel represented and recognized. Generally, this type of congregation is not very large because it has to dedicate much of its energy to the process of effective interaction among the various groups.[3]

Congregations in Transition

In areas going through demographic transition, one can find churches that decide to be proactive in ministering to the new ethnic community moving into the area. Many times these are denominationally directed projects. This often begins by seeking out a Latina pastor who is bilingual and bicultural. This person provides pastoral care to the congregation that is in decline, while she works to establish a Latino congregation. The goal is to continue supporting the declining group while a new congregation is established. In some cases this also involves making changes in the English-language congregation so that it can minister more effectively to Latinos who prefer an English-language service.

Another variant of the model is one where the group in decline transfers its building to the Latino congregation. This allows the building to continue being used to minister in the community, even though the population has changed.

In theory this model provides a way to continue using the building to minister in the community. But in practice it can create many intercultural tensions. Many times a majority culture congregation in decline already feels threatened by the changes occurring in their community. So working in this type of transitional model can feel like a threat to the only thing they still "control." This model is a good

> In our particular situation, the biggest challenge has been trying to maintain the vision of an intercultural and holistic ministry, notwithstanding the opposition of a handful of elderly people of majority culture [who are] full of fear of losing control over what they consider to be their property, the church building.
>
> ROBERTO COLÓN

strategy at the denominational level because it provides an opportunity to continue using buildings to minister in the community in which they were built. But it also demands a great deal of preparatory work and training in intercultural relations so that the result is one in which everyone can feel that he or she is doing God's work.

Ministry Models, Theological Perspectives, and Missional Churches

Much has been written about the theological and missiological implications of the various models of church and ministry we have been describing. No attempt will be made to address the issue, even less to resolve it, in this next section. Nonetheless, it is important to recognize that each one of the models previously described has ecclesiological and missiological implications that need to be taken into account.

The church growth movement said that churches grow best when they are monocultural. Many have questioned the theological basis of homogeneous units and have argued that the biblical model of church is one in which people of different cultures worship God together and that this needs to be the model for today, even if it makes it more difficult to establish churches.

Latino churches find themselves in a complex situation in relationship to this issue. Outsiders see them as monocultural,

79

and some denominations and movements have started Latino ministries based on their understanding of the homogeneous church growth principle. Nonetheless, many Latino congregations are multicultural, with people from many countries, cultures, and backgrounds. These congregations are not seen this way by those on the outside, who many times only see "Latinas," a category that for them is monocultural.

The biblical model presents churches crossing cultural and linguistic boundaries. Many Latino churches are already multicultural; yet they need to be more intentional in their willingness to work with people from different cultures, whether these are from Latin America or from the Latino subcultures in the United States. If the Latino church is going to take its missional responsibility seriously, it needs to find ways to minister among non-Latinos. The challenge is to find models in which the Latino church can be intentionally multicultural within Latino complexity, even as it seeks ways to be a missional church in conjunction with congregations from other ethnic or cultural backgrounds.

> The majority of Latino churches need to offer programs and ministries in both languages with a tint of the cultural *mestizaje* that is part of Latino communities.
>
> EDUARDO FONT

Ministering to the Vast Array of Community Needs

Latino churches are responding and need to continue to respond to the vast needs of the Latino community as they focus on the missional responsibility of the church. Some of the major missional themes have particular resonance in the Latino community.

Reconciliation

One of the key words used in the Bible to describe what God is doing through Christ is *reconciliation*. This is a crucial theme within the Latina community. First of all, we confess that we need reconciliation with God through Jesus Christ. But we also recognize that the community needs various types of reconciliation.

Latinos need to work toward the reconciliation of dysfunctional family systems, between Latino subcultures, between generations, between immigrants and those born in the United States, between social classes, and in the many other divisions we have created in the Latino community or that have been imposed on us by the majority society. We also need to work toward reconciliation between Latinos and other minority groups in the United States, particularly African Americans. On the other hand, we need to find new models of interaction with the majority society that include reconciliation processes.

A specific area in which the Latino church needs to foment reconciliation is related to *machismo*. Our people have practiced and justified unjust treatment of women for generations. Domestic violence is all too common, even in our churches and among our Latino *evangélico* leaders. Many Latino churches have also limited the ministry of women, even though they are the majority in almost all Latino churches and they are the ones who work the hardest to support Latino churches. Without getting into theological questions that some Latino leaders might raise related to this subject, it is clear that reconciliation between women and men is a topic that the Latino church needs to address, be it in church, family, or Latino culture in general.

By focusing on reconciliation ministries, Latino churches are recognizing the divine call and also the reality of human need. The ministry of reconciliation has to include the proclamation and invitation to reconcile with God through Jesus Christ. This ministry also has to include the task and commitment of working toward reconciliation in all of the areas previously mentioned. The church needs to be at the vanguard of the reconciliation process, particularly in those barrios and communities where the encounter between our people and other ethnic groups has been full of tensions and difficulties.

Latino churches are already working to develop models of reconciliation within the family and between the different Latino cultures. The next step is for Latino churches to work

81

toward intercultural reconciliation that will reflect the gospel that we preach.

Community

One of the most common messages heard in Latino churches is that of church as community. The churches serve as support to immigrants who are far from their family ties, those who have moved to a new location in search of better opportunities, those who have separated from their families due to problems, and still many others among us who find themselves alone. Because of our cultural particularities, this is one of the ministries that the majority of Latino churches find easier to do. Many people find a network of relations in Latino churches that support them in various aspects of being family, that provide the support and encouragement that they need, and a circle of friends who help them find employment, housing, and other types of help.

> I think that every person that arrives from another country needs to have a place and feel like they are a part of a place that has components of their home and family. This is where the church can begin [its ministry].
>
> CLEMENTINA CHACÓN

This asset of many Latino churches will continue being more and more indispensable for the Latino community. The churches will need to be proactive in the process of providing support, training members of the church to see how they place themselves at the service of those who seek, and desperately need, community.

This idea of church as community also implies supporting the development and strengthening of community systems. The communities where Latinas live often do not have many public services, or these services are deficient, at best. The church as community also takes seriously the importance of working with other churches to develop a holistic ministry that creates community and to support community service structures.

82

An important concept in the gospel is hope. Believing in the future is indispensable in the Latino community; our religiosity helps us believe that God becomes present in our lives. In some of our communities, however, to believe

> When we talk about specific goals we always do it understanding that God has called us as a church to extend the Kingdom of God through our practice of compassion, promotion of peace, justice and spirituality, even as we struggle against systemic poverty in collaboration with other churches, educational agencies and community social services.
>
> ROBERTO COLÓN

in God is to believe that the current situation has no possibility of change, which is a kind of fatalism. Our churches need to foster hope. We believe in the future because God worked in the past and continues working today. This is a message we need to proclaim, but it is also a call to action. The immigrant arrives with hope. But the circumstances immigrants face in this country many times end up weakening or

> For me the most important issue is for the church to see itself as part of the society around us. Having grown up in the Latino church in this country I realize that we were so afraid of worldly things that we ignored what was happening in the community and we lost many opportunities to have an impact with the gospel and transformative message of Jesus.
>
> JAMES ORTIZ

destroying that hope. The churches that are working in these areas are helping open up opportunities for education and preparation so that people can visualize a future in this country. These churches are also working to call their members to be sources of hope for those around them.

A specific area in which the church needs to foster hope is in relationship to just and comprehensive immigration reform. Historically, the vast majority of Latino pastors have avoided political participation, believing that it is not the church's place

83

to get involved in issues that are not specifically "spiritual." There has always been a minority of Latino pastors willing to struggle with political issues, particularly pastors from more liberal denominations. Recently, some Latino *evangélico* leaders from more conservative movements have begun to address issues like abortion or homosexual marriage. But the issue of immigration reform has persuaded many Latino pastors of the importance of their political participation.

> My role is to be prophetic on this issue and to be ready to advocate in relationship to the immigration situation so that the way we think about and do the work of the Kingdom will change.
>
> WALTER CONTRERAS

Many Latino churches have lived the contradiction of preaching about the importance of "obeying" legal authorities, appealing to a very limited interpretation of Romans 13, and during prayer time interceding for the person who is going to "cross tonight." Many Latino pastors have opted to ignore the implications of receiving the tithes of the undocumented, even as they preach against undocumented migration.

This issue took on new importance for many Latino pastors at the end of 2005 when the House of Representatives approved HR 4437, a proposal that would have criminalized helping the undocumented. They now have a new vision of the importance of working in the political arena on behalf of Latinos and others who need to get out of the shadows and into legality.

> We Latinos need a larger cause to unite us. I believe that the Spirit of God is actively working today in our communities to unite us around the issue of immigration.
>
> ROBERTO COLÓN

Since an immigration reform law was not approved in 2007, some Latino churches are preparing for the elections, while others are participating in testimonial actions like the New

84

Sanctuary Movement. It is yet to be seen whether the issue of immigration reform will serve to unite Latino pastors to work together to influence political processes in favor of other needs within the community.

Identity

One of the great challenges confronting the Latino community, particularly the young people, is the issue of identity: who am I? We Latinos receive conflicting messages, including many that denigrate or devalue our Latino identity. The Latino church becomes a place where we can celebrate who we are as sons and daughters of God and what we can contribute to God and to our world as Latinas. The Latino church provides the place for us to celebrate our polycentric identity before God. We are not talking of cultural pride but of a positive identity that helps us participate in the public life in our society.

> We need to help people find an identity that allows them to express all their potential, develop equal relations with other minorities and social classes, and take a more visible role in leadership in business, education, and politics.
> PABLO ANABALÓN

In the midst of the displacement of the immigrant and the lack of a clear identity faced by many in our community, the church provides us with a place where we can celebrate our walking before God as Latinos as a divine gift. This gives us the basis to grow and to also develop a transformative identity that takes us beyond the humanly imposed limitations toward what God wants to develop in us.

> The church needs to become a culture creator, not merely a countercultural movement.
> OSCAR & KARLA GARCÍA

Latino theologians have invited us to recognize various aspects of our identity as gifts that allow us to read the Bible and understand God's work in the world in a particular way. **85**

> As part of our community work, beyond the message of the grace of God that transforms lives, we teach English, and we prepare adults to graduate from high school. We do not promote assimilation but we do promote full integration in Anglo Saxon culture. We teach and motivate people to buy homes, develop roots, and not move from place to place. We encourage people to train themselves to obtain better jobs and to move up the economic ladder. We want people to move from employee to their employer's partner, then to employer, paying just wages, working with a Christian ethic.
>
> JUAN CARLOS ORTIZ

These aspects are a gift to us, but also something that we can share so that others may learn about our particular encounter with God. Justo González suggests that we can learn from our experiences of *mestizaje*, marginality, poverty, exile, and solidarity. Each one of these concepts describes parts of our reality:

• We are a people who came into existence in the encounter (many times forced) between peoples.
• We cannot claim any racial "purity."
• Many Latinas live on the margins of US society.
• The level of poverty among Latinas is high.
• Many Latinos feel displaced, even many of those whose family has been living in the United States for several generations.

Nonetheless, in the midst of this we are a people who have learned to stand in solidarity with our own. In the midst of these experiences, we have learned that God walks with the little ones and the marginalized, with the poor and displaced, and that God wants us to form a new people.

Latino churches that want to have a positive impact on Latino identity are using Latino experiences as a starting point to help the community understand that God wants to be present among us. These churches are helping to answer the question: what does it means to be a disciple of Jesus Christ from within my multifaceted Latino reality?

Tools for Life

Many members of the Latino community need tools to function effectively in US society. Some need basic things like nutritious food, training to obtain decent employment, safe housing, and education for them and for their children. Some also need training to understand how to function in US society. The Latino community is already contributing greatly

> Independent churches, in particular, show mixed and particular cultural genes. These congregations have mixed together various elements and have created their own culture somewhat different from their previous ones. Not only have they maintained Latin American cultural traits and also Anglo Saxon cultural traits, many times they have also generated a distinctive ecclesial mestizaje, a third social reality. They have created religious culture.
>
> OSCAR & KARLA GARCÍA

to this country, but it has the potential of having a much greater impact, with the right tools. Churches can participate in the training and also serve as a bridge between the people and organizations that provide the training programs.

Churches can also help develop positive relations between spouses, parents and children, families, churches, and communities. Many churches provide seminars, workshops, retreats, and other types of activities to support the Latino family. If healthy families develop, the Latino community will be strengthened.

Latinos also need ways to interpret US reality from a Christian perspective. It is too easy for many Latinos to interpret the situation in this country only in positive or in negative terms, without being able to analyze the complexities of the impact of US culture. Churches can help immigrant believers learn to theologically read the situation that made them immigrate and those who were born in this country to understand the complex context in which they live. Latinos need to be able to interpret globalization and recognize the need to contribute to and to question the current situation.

87

Models of Interdependent Ministry

When my parents were preparing for ministry at a Spanish-language Bible Institute in south Texas during the 1960s, our family faced many needs. They had sensed God's call to ministry within the Latino community and had moved from California to Texas to study in a Spanish-language institution. Our financial situation was very difficult and the small Latino church my parents were pastoring barely provided enough to pay the rent, much less buy food and cover other expenses. In the midst of that situation a person gave my father the following advice: "Join the god of the gringos. The god of the Mexicans does not pay."

This type of economic disparity has existed in US/Latino ministry since Protestant mission work began in the nineteenth century. The churches of majority culture have the financial resources, the trained personnel, the buildings, the vision, and the disposition. The majority of Latino churches are poor and their members almost always have fewer economic resources than the members of other churches. Because of this financial disparity, situations of economic dependence or codependence have often developed between many Latino churches and majority culture churches. In some denominations these codependent relations have existed for decades and it seems as if they can never change, no matter how much people seek to change them.

Codependency has its roots in the economic inequality that we need to confront as Christians. It develops because of the perspective we have about money and ministry. In the rich churches of the first world, there is the temptation to define ministry growth around money. Money becomes the principal resource when it comes time to talk about doing mission. Other resources, like spiritual gifts, human effort, vision, or a willingness to work, are seen as secondary to money. So ministry is defined around budgets and those who have the money define the ministry. The capacity to go forward becomes dependent on denominational decisions or on the churches or people of majority culture that have the economic resources or access to them.[4]

This tends to create uncomfortable relations for everyone involved. Economic codependency upsets both those who give and those who are dependent on the economic resources of others. But it also tends to hurt the Latino ministry or church in that these never become completely responsible for their own local ministry. Many Latino churches in the United States continue receiving some outside economic subsidy twenty, thirty, or even fifty years after being established. Other Latino churches have disappeared or have cut their ties to their denominational roots because of economic problems rooted in codependency. Denominations that once had a large number of Latino congregations have limited impact in the Latino community today.

In many cases we see an inverse relationship between the amount of money invested and the development of a strong Latino church. The more money that is invested, the more difficult it is to establish strong ministries in which the members of the church become economically responsible for themselves.

It is not easy to change this type of situation. Both the one who gives and the one who receives have become used to certain patterns and relationships and they tend to interpret their reality in a way that justifies it and makes it difficult to change it. In this "picture" the Latino is always the "poor" person who cannot take responsibility for his own future and the people of majority culture are the "saviors" who can feel good about what they are doing on behalf of the needy. Latinos complain about the control of people from outside, and the "Anglos" feel like people are taking

> Our goal is to establish Latino churches led by Latino leaders that do not need to be dependent on Americans but where Latinos can become owners of their own buildings. We want to create the capacity in our Latino leaders in the area of compassion and justice ministries so that they can assume civic, social and spiritual responsibilities as leaders in their communities.
>
> WALTER CONTRERAS

advantage of them. Both lament their "role" without finding a way out.

Obviously, Latinas, even poor Latinas, can develop and sustain their own churches. They are doing it every day throughout the United States. But it is also important to recognize that the biblical vision goes beyond self-sufficient churches to interdependent congregations that reflect a united church demonstrating the divine vision of a community of all people, ethnicities, languages, and cultures united by Jesus Christ (Revelation 7:8-9). Christian churches of various cultural backgrounds need to learn to work together in such a way that they will provide a testimony of unity and also wisely use their resources to minister effectively in our world.

The economic disparities between rich and poor churches will always complicate any effort to develop economic independence and joint work among equals. Nonetheless, it is important today to develop new types of relations between financially strong churches and those with fewer economic resources. These new relations will imply changes for both sides. Latino churches need to define our own place within US society and in relationship to majority culture churches. We also need to celebrate and use the resources God has given us. Latino churches have gifts, disposition, vision, and know the power of God that manifests itself in real life. They have accomplished much with what they have, and we must not diminish the value of all this. The economic system in which we live wants to persuade us that the most important resource in ministry is money. We need to confront this lie and call the church and US society to break its captivity to money.

Majority culture churches need to confront the implicit racism in any codependent relationship. This problem does not

> Latino leaders need to quit being afraid of "white" leadership and need to represent the Latino community with courage, firmness, and humility. Many leaders do not know how to talk when in the midst of White dominant leadership. They tend to be pleasant and not honest.
>
> JOSÉ GARCÍA

only exist in the United States. It affects the service ministries and projects of many churches and service agencies around the world. The best intentions will only have a positive effect if there is a change in attitude in the rich benefactor toward the "poor" poor people. Those who have economic resources need to recognize that they are merely administrators and that God is inviting them to use what they have to bless others. They also need to break with their captivity to money through a generous responsibility.

As we bring together the resources of Latino churches with those of majority culture churches, and those of other minority churches, we can dream of developing churches with interdependent relationships. These relationships depend on believing that it is God who calls us to work together toward God's future. Latina churches are already doing a lot to respond to the needs of the Latino community and beyond. As we join efforts in interdependence, we will be able to multiply our ministries for the glory of God and for the benefit of the country in which we live.

> We believe that the only way to work together is, first of all, to "demythologize" the concept and practice of "unity." We believe that there is great potential in the Latino concept of *convivencia* [life together]. Theologically speaking *convivencia* is the capacity to live together through Christ and because of Christ, following Dietrich Bonhoeffer's logic.
>
> OSCAR & KARLA GARCÍA

5

Ministering for Today and for Tomorrow

We live in the midst of profound worldwide change. Globalization and postmodernity are changing all the categories that we thought we knew and understood. These changes are having an impact on the Latina community and will affect our future in this country. We cannot speak of future ministry in the Latino community without taking into account that we are immersed in this larger reality. Nonetheless, the Latino community also has a series of particularities with which it has to deal as it plans toward the future. Specifically, Latino *evangélico* churches need to think about ministry to their young people, the formation of leaders for the Latino churches of the future, new models of ministry, and the ability to understand the "signs of the times" in relationship to the Latino community.

Ministering to Latino Young People

Youth ministry has always been a challenge to the church.[1] Every generation questions the previous one and seeks to walk in new directions. Young people in each generation have to struggle with their identity formation in the midst of a complexity of influences, all of which want to shape them into "their own image." For Latino young people these influences include church, family, and community. But there are also the **93**

> The second generation is always an afterthought, not the principal concern of the group. The struggle to maintain Latino identity while we learn the best of the culture in which we live offers us many opportunities, but we need the support of others [in this process].
>
> ALEXIA SALVATIERRA

powerful influences of globalized youth culture, mass media, and social communication networks. Our young people are being formed and are creating their identity in the midst of all of these influences; and it is the work of the church, family, and community to accompany them as they develop into mature adults committed to following the way of Jesus Christ.

> The worldview of the generations is also different, so Latino leaders need to have ministries directed to each generation.
>
> SERGIO NAVARRETE

We must remember that Latino young people present all the diversities previously mentioned related to the Latino community in general. But in the midst of all that diversity one has to add the fact that they are being formed and educated in the midst of US youth culture. They are under much more pressure to assimilate into majority culture than Latino adults, but they are also seeking ways to develop their identity as Latino young people. In this process it seems that they are simultaneously fleeing from, seeking out, and reforming their Latino identity. To be able to minister effectively among them, one needs to take into account this complexity that is the life of Latino adolescents and young adults.

> I believe that each generation approaches God according to its own need and the reasons for which the parents are looking for God and hope are not the same reasons for which their children are looking.
>
> CLEMENTINA CHACÓN

Latino churches need to take the time to understand the complex experience of the young people in their churches and to develop ministries and support systems that respond to these complexities. The first of these experiences has to do with the place where they were formed. Those who were born or raised in the United States and those who immigrated as young people have clear differences between them. These differences have to do with values and worldview, not merely with language. With US-born young people one also has to take into account the formation they have received from their parents. Some were raised with a strong Latino identity, while other parents have wanted their children to "Americanize." These formative differences begin to define the types of differences one sees among Latina youth.

Instituto Fe y Vida, a project of the La Salle Brothers of the Catholic Church in the United States, has identified four broad "types" of Latino youth within the Catholic churches in this country. They use these four categories to help those who are doing pastoral work among young people to understand that the Latino youth that go to their churches will have very different needs and interests. These are not exclusive categories but rather descriptions of tendencies that one can observe among Latino young people. If we superimpose those categories on the diagram that we used previously to describe the cultural identification of the Latino community, we can chart the various categories proposed by Instituto Fe y Vida in the following manner:

Figure 5A
Types of identification of Latino youth[2]

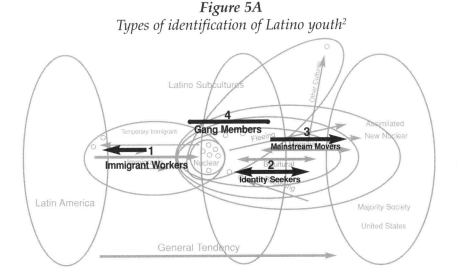

Immigrant workers are Latino youth who emigrated from Latin America somewhat recently. They received their formation and education in their countries of origin and they maintain strong ties to the South. Many of these young people do not have much formal education, though some of them arrive from Latin America with a great deal of education. This type of young person has a clear Latino/Latin American identity. If she has been a part of a church in her country of origin, she expects youth activities that look like those she experienced "over there." This young person's participation in globalized youth culture tends to be through Latino or Latin American portals. Many of these young people are or will become fully bilingual and bicultural as the years go by.

Identity seekers generally are young people who have been born or raised in the United States. As adolescents and young adults they are trying to find their own cultural space. Many of them are experimenting with aspects of Latino culture, majority culture, and maybe even other cultural expressions. They want to celebrate aspects of their Latino identity, but they are mixing them with other influences they are receiving from other sources. What this type of young person most needs is space to experiment and reformulate their cultural identity.

The church needs to provide expressions of both languages in daily life. This is a magnificent opportunity to train young leaders, born and/or raised in this country, so that they can develop ministry among the second, third, or fourth generation that prefer English outside of the home. In our particular context it is very important that the pastor and leaders be bilingual because our young people, though they can understand Spanish, constantly change languages in their conversations.

ROBERTO COLÓN

Mainstream movers are young people who are clearly on their way to majority society. Their understanding of the future is related to fully participating in majority culture. Generally they have limited identification with their Latino roots and see little reason to identify with things Latino. The roots of this tendency might be the formation they

96

received from their parents or the influence of important people in their lives. Many of these young people will go to college and their Latino identity will be of minimal importance. They anticipate that their future will be on the margins or completely outside of the Latino community.

The last category, *gang members*, reflects the reality of Latino young people who got lost between their parents' culture and majority culture. These young persons do not feel that they fit in any other space, so they seek their identity and community among the gang members. The gang ends up providing what society has taken away or, at least, has not adequately provided.

Ministry among Latino youth is complicated not only because of these diverse reasons, but also because parents are not always in agreement about what they want for their children. Many parents want the church to be a place where their children can affirm their Latino identity and where they can use and improve their Spanish. Nonetheless, others want their children to "Americanize" so that they do not "suffer" as they have suffered as they incorporated into US reality. These parents want their children to participate in youth programs that will prepare them to be good "Americans."

One can see this ambivalence in issues of language and social participation. Some parents want their children to speak Spanish well and others prefer they not even learn it. This reflects the different perspectives previously mentioned about the place of Latinas in majority society. Some want to foment a bicultural and bilingual identity in their children, while others envision the future as a complete assimilation into majority culture.[3]

The conflicting opinions of the parents complicate the work of the church because there is no "neutral" position. The church has to ask itself what message it wants to communicate to its young people. If it organizes activities with a Latino focus, it is communicating that it is important to maintain a Latino identity. If it does not, it communicates that it believes in assimilation. The position taken by the church will affect the **97** type of ministry and also the role of the church as a social agent.

The position put forth in this book is that the best way for Latino young people to develop wings to participate in their world is to develop strong roots of cultural identification. Though the previous sentence mixes metaphors, it is a useful description of the result we aim for. The goal is to help Latino young people strengthen their Christian and Latino identity, something that will allow them to broaden their identity in order to have a positive impact in the world.

To reach this goal, the Latino church needs to remember that the gospel always develops in concrete cultures. The church has the responsibility of sharing the gospel, calling people to it, and forming disciples of Jesus Christ. But this process always has to occur in concrete cultural contexts, in this case, Latino reality. Latino young people will be able to affirm their confession of faith in Christ with more clarity to the extent that this confession is done from an affirmation of their Latino identity.

> The church needs to develop communication bridges between the different generations, and to develop leaders that can serve a more questioning and exacting generation.
>
> MARIBEL ZACAPA

In this perspective, the Latino church will be an important place to celebrate and affirm Latino cultures. Latino reality is seen in a negative way or in an extremely superficial way in many US contexts. The Spanish language is attacked or devalued in many circles. Many people continue to claim that the Latino presence is a danger to the national identity of the United States.[4]

Our young people need a more positive presentation of what it means to be Latino. They do not need an idealism that denies the negative parts of our culture. They do need a different reading of Latino history and of the

> Another way we are trying to help our young people is by tellling them that it is all right to speak Spanish.
>
> SAÚL & ROSAMARÍA MALDONADO

riches of Latina culture. Alongside this reading they also need tools to interpret their Latino experience in the United States. They need to begin to think about globalization processes and about migratory movements that have shaped today's Latino community.

Another important function of the church is the celebration of the Spanish language. This language is an important part of Latino identity and a means for worshiping God together across generations. The purpose of teaching Spanish to our children is not only for cultural identification, it is also an invitation to our young people to see the

> We need to listen to our young people a lot. We need to give them a platform, a space to be able to speak. I find myself asking them, what are we missing?
>
> ADELITA GARZA

world through a broader vision. The United States has developed and almost celebrated a monolingualism that has limited the influence it can have in a globalized world. Encouraging the learning of Spanish is to prepare our children for the future, a future increasingly multicultural and multilingual.

The Latino church needs to open options to young people so that they can grow as people and as Christians. As she gets to understand the gospel and begins to serve in her community, the young Latina begins to understand her reason for being in this world. The church also presents options when it opens opportunities for positive contact with Latin America by means of mission and service projects. This gives young people opportunities to see their parents' or ancestors' countries of origin through more realistic eyes, instead of through the often-negative interpretations in the US mass media.

All of this process needs to occur in a context where young people have the liberty to experiment and decide about their identity. Some moments a young person will identify with what is Latino and other times he will try to deny anything Latino. Those who work with young people will need to understand that this is part of the process of identity formation and that the church needs to be a safe place where he can **99**

> Our church will confront the problem of disconnect with the young people of the second and third generation. Since we do not have a model for youth ministry or a clear understanding of how to minister to new generations, my fear is that we will end up with churches of elderly people and eventually decline because of the lack of new blood and [a failure] to reach emerging generations.
>
> DANNY MARTÍNEZ

experiment with the different options that his world presents. The church also needs to be a place where he feels support as he makes decisions about his future, even though the young person might decide that his Latino identity may not have much to offer for the future.

The principal goal of work with young people is to help them become citizens of the divine Kingdom that is not limited to any specific human culture. We want to help them define and strengthen their Christian commitment no matter where their lives take them. They need to hear a transcultural gospel, one born in Latino reality but that goes far beyond. What we are looking for is that they may live as citizens of the Kingdom wherever God may lead them. The goal of youth ministry, and of Latino ministry in general, needs to be to form Christians for a globalized world.

Some Latino churches proclaim that their church is the church of their sons and daughters. This type of statement carried some weight in a more stable social situation. Of course we want to communicate to our daughters and sons that they have a special place in the life of our congregations. But the reality of movement and social changes in our world means that the majority of our children will not likely be a part of our churches. Some will remain near our churches and might be a part of the next generation of members of our congregations. But the majority will go to other places. As they move, some will seek to be members of other Latino churches. Others will go to non-Latino churches. We will have fulfilled our task if they go with a clear identity as followers of Jesus Christ.[5]

100

Training the Next Generation of Leaders

As we approach the topic of the training of a new generation of leaders for Latino *evangélico* churches, we need to be clear about both the recruiting process and the formational process. Since the Latino community is so diverse and the need for leaders will continue to grow, it is important to recognize that the leaders will come from many different places and the challenges of training them will be as complex as is the community.

Seeking out New Leaders

Currently, future Latino pastors are coming from three principal sources. On the one hand, many immigrant churches are looking

> The immigrant Latino pastor needs to know that what works in Chiapas may not work in Chatsworth.
>
> JIM TOLLE

for their leaders in Latin America. The migratory flow is such that it is not difficult to find pastors or leaders in Latin America willing to serve among the Latino community in the United States. Also, many pastors migrating from Latin America are looking for any employment opportunity and decide to re-take up ministry. Many of these pastors come with extensive ministry experience, but very few of them have worked in a transcultural environment, which means that they are almost never prepared for the specific task of working with the Latino community here. These pastors go through the same cultural adjustments and the same adaptation issues as any other immigrant. This makes it easier for them to identify themselves with the situation faced by other immigrants, but this can limit their effectiveness if they are not trained to understand what is happening and to identify the differences between ministering among Latinos in this country and ministry in Latin America.

A second important source of pastors for Latino churches are lay leaders who develop within Latino churches. These people have a strong Christian commitment and have developed **101** within the life of the church. Generally they have jobs or businesses and families. However, many of these lay leaders do not have a great deal of formal education. This makes it difficult to prepare them for ministry using traditional US educational systems. Some denominations limit the ministry opportunities of people who do not have much formal education. This creates situations where people with a strong sense of call, commitment, and impact in the Latino community can never be ordained or fully recognized by their denominations.

The traditional source for identifying leaders in the US context has been the young people who are trained from a young age for ministry as vocation and profession. Latino churches have also identified young people for ministry. But the result for Latino churches has often depended on the place where they have been trained. Latino young people who have gone to traditional seminaries many times have ended up "dislocated" in relationship to the Latino community. Latino Bible Institutes have had more "success" in training young people for Latino ministry, though the graduates have almost always ended up with a nonaccredited diploma or degree.

These sources of Latino leaders have also produced people who are ministering beyond the Latino community. As Latino churches continue recruiting future pastors and leaders, they will also need to take into account the importance of identifying men and women from the community whose ministries will develop beyond the Latino community. The Latino church is not only producing leaders for its churches; it is also sending its leaders to serve in other contexts.

> We Latino pastors need to be generalists. We need to know a little about many things because we are asked to answer questions and to respond to needs of the people as lawyers, accountants, doctors, and immigration experts. I believe that the Latino leader needs to understand what is happening beyond the church and the Bible. There is a need to expose oneself to what exists in the community and to develop relationships with community resources. One needs to have a broad understanding of one's ministry.
>
> JAMES ORTIZ

Figure 5B
Perfect Latino pastor

The Types of Leaders Needed

The ideal Latina pastor has a clear sense of divine call and has demonstrated it in the life of the church. She is completely bilingual (oral and written), understands the complexities of the Latino community, has training in intercultural relations, and has transnational experience. She has a theological formation that includes biblical, theological, ministerial, and transcultural knowledge, understands the importance of the church having a missional perspective, and knows how to minister in the midst of the changes of a globalized world. She also

103

needs to be a person willing to live among the people to effectively minister in an incarnational way.

Of course, the problem is that ideals are exactly that, ideals toward which we point, recognizing that it is very difficult to reach all of them. Nonetheless, the ideal points to several important things. On the one hand, many people have most of these capacities, but they are never fully recognized for what they can do. On the other hand, the ideal points toward very real needs in the community and to the challenge of preparing people to be able to minister in this complexity.

> From my perspective, many of us are receiving our formation as leaders and our recognition outside of Latino churches. After that, we return as prodigal children to contribute what we have learned—but we are not always welcomed.
>
> ALEXIA SALVATIERRA

The challenge is to identify the leaders and also to prepare them to serve in a context where they will need to do a bit of everything. Whoever is not ready to be a "generalist" is going to have a hard time ministering effectively in the Latino community.

Historically, Latino pastors have been formed in one of three different ways or in a combination of the three. Many of the pastors have been formed in the practice of ministry, with some mentorship, but have never received any formal training. Some of these people have formal education in some other area, but many are self-educated. This type of pastor is seeking to form himself "on the job" by means of seminars, workshops, and other nonformal means.

Some pastors have been educated in US seminaries. Generally, these people pastor churches that require a Master of Divinity degree for ordination. These pastors have a high level of education, since most seminaries require an academic degree (B.A. or equivalent) and a high level of English-language usage. Some denominations provide scholarships for seminary studies. But the costs and the prerequisites have limited the number of Latinos that graduate from seminaries. **104** Another problem has been that few seminaries have programs or courses that train these people for the specific challenges of ministry in the Latino community. Certain mistrust has also developed between Latino leaders who have studied in US seminaries and those who have not, to the extent that some seminary graduates have found barriers to ministry in the community when they return.

A smaller group of Latino pastors has been trained in seminaries in Latin America. These people come with a solid biblical and theological formation, but they have been trained to minister in a similar, but different, context. They can fulfill denominational requirements for ordination but then have to struggle with the problems faced by any other immigrant pastor who ministers in this country.

Many Latino pastors have been formed in nonaccredited Bible Institutes, particularly those in the Pentecostal or independent arena. The institutes vary a great deal as to academic level or quality of training. Some have very solid programs and offer several formational opportunities. Others have very limited programs and very inferior academic levels. The Bible Institutes have the advantage that they can be much more flexible in relationship to academic prerequisites they set for the students and also in relationship to modes of delivery. Many are able to adapt very well to the specific needs of their students and are very economical when compared to the costs of formal programs. That is why so many people study in them.

Nonetheless, Bible Institutes present several challenges, particularly related to issues of accreditation. Since they are not part of accrediting associations, their diplomas and degrees have no academic recognition, something that limits their value beyond the life of the church. The lack of accreditation also limits the opportunities for these programs to have an evaluation process that assures the quality of the education.[6]

The challenges of training become more complex when one takes into account the immigrant pastors who were formed in Latin America. These people reflect all of the variety previously mentioned but with the additional challenge of arriving with a formation that trained them to minister in a context very different from the Latino reality in the United States. They also

105

struggle with the fact that the systems of formation in Latin America are very different from those in the United States, and it is not always easy to "translate" their academic formation so that those who wish to can continue their theological studies in this country.[7] Another challenge that immigrant pastors face is one we have already mentioned; they are struggling with their own adaptation to this country even as they are attempting to guide their members in that same task.

As the Latino community continues to grow, the challenges for training sufficient pastors and leaders for Latino churches will continue to grow. This need is creating new spaces for the formation of future pastors. Among US seminaries, a growing number have developed programs for nontraditional students, people without previous academic degrees or who already have families and commitments that make it impossible for them to dedicate themselves to full-time study or to move to another city to study. Some seminaries are also providing programs or courses in Spanish and some seminaries also are requiring Spanish as a "ministry language." Nonetheless, the impact of accredited seminaries continues to be limited. Today, Latinos comprise almost 15 percent of the population of the country but account for less than 4 percent of the students in US seminaries.[8]

New Bible Institutes continue being opened throughout the country. Though they vary in quality and academic level, they are responding to this great need. Some institutions and denominations have recognized the value of Bible Institutes and are working now to strengthen their programs and to link them to accredited institutions. Some seminaries and uni-

> Tomorrow's Latino leaders will need, first of all, to know their roots very well, their culture, their history, understanding their own identity, so that they can offer solutions to the sociocultural issues that are coming, leaders capable of understanding their people and advocating for the needs of the Latino people. We need leaders conscious of the complexities of each generation but willing to find communication bridges.
>
> MARIBEL ZACAPA

versities are working alongside the institutes to open up possibilities to the graduates so that they can continue studying in accredited institutions.[9]

Projects like the Asociación para la Educación Teológica Hispana (AETH) (Association for Hispanic Theological Education) and the Asociación Teológica Hispana (ATH) (Hispanic Theological Association) of southern California are helping support the work of the institutes by means of producing materials, training directors and professors, and providing systems for evaluation and recognition, though not formal accreditation. Also a few Latino Bible Institutes have opted to work toward formal accreditation. The process is long and difficult, but a few institutes have obtained accreditation.

Any program will need to take into account what type of leader it wants to form. This decision will be affected by theological and denominational perspectives and also by the perspective on the Latino community and its place in US society. Nonetheless, the formation programs need to identify people who the community recognizes as leaders, or future leaders, and who have a clear sense of call or vocation for ministry. Any program that is going to be successful will need to be flexible, taking into account the particularities of the majority of Latinos and of the Latino community. They will need to broaden the concept of mission and ministry to respond in a holistic way to Latino reality. In the majority of cases, they will need to train people so that they can function well in both Spanish and English and so that they can understand the complexity of the Latino experience. It will probably need to include ministry experience in Latin America for those Latinas born or raised in the United States. And a good program will also need to provide tools to interpret Latino experience in the midst of the changes

> We need to work from our strengths and not lament our weaknesses. We have great Latino pastors that do not speak English and are doing very good work.
>
> WALTER CONTRERAS

107

occurring at a global level and their implications for the mission of the church.

> My biggest challenge definitely is being a single Latina pastor. I confront challenges when I counsel men, fathers, and couples. I recognize that I need to connect myself with people who have experience being married.
>
> ADELITA GARZA

We also need to recognize that God uses people who do not always have all the tools we would like them to have. We should not be afraid to work with and support men and women who have many limitations but who have a strong commitment to ministry and to the Latino community.

Latino *evangélico* churches also need to address the issue of women in ministry. The majority of our churches are part of traditions that affirm the ministry of women. Nonetheless, in practice the majority of Latinas who are pastors have found many barriers in the community. We are open to having women as co-pastors with their husbands. But God is raising up women as principal leaders and we need to rethink our models of pastoral ministry in the Latino community. A particular challenge for the Latino church is the population of young single Latinas who are training for ministry and have much to offer the church. They are being used by God. The challenge will be whether the Latino church will know how to receive this gift.

New Models of Church and Ministry

The growing diversity that we have been describing invites us to continue looking for new ways of being church and of doing mission in the Latina community. Some of the models that will be mentioned are already beginning to be used. We have yet to see whether these will be the models that will respond to the specific needs of the community. What we do need to recognize is that these models address real situations among Latinos, situations that cannot be ignored if we want to minister effectively in the community.

A specific group of people make up a situation that is being lived in the midst of Latino migratory movements: people who move from south to north and north to south various times during their lives. Many of these people identify themselves as *evangélicas,* and they want to be part of a church in the place where they live. But they also have links to churches in more than one place and country. Some churches and denominations have developed a more transnational concept of the church in which they can provide pastoral support no matter where they are. This support varies from place to place. Some follow their members until they are established in another church; others maintain a communication link between churches and pastors. What is developing in some cases is a type of *transnational church* that recognizes that it continues having a pastoral responsibility for its people, and that, in some cases, this support has to be given by several congregations in more than one country working together. The periodic movement and transnational lifestyle of many people will make it indispensable to develop a pastoral accompaniment that crosses national borders and the walls of individual churches.

A variant of the transnational church is a *migrant church.* In years past there were Latino pastors who followed their members when they went out on migratory labor routes, mostly for agricultural work. Today the migratory patterns of many people are not nearly as defined as of those who worked in the fields. Nonetheless, there is a need for pastors and leaders willing to accompany people in their migratory movements. This implies rethinking the concept of church from being linked to a geographic location to church as tied to a group of people, no matter where they may be found.

We have already mentioned that many Latino churches are multicultural because they have people of several countries and various ethnic backgrounds. What needs to grow is the number of Latino churches that develop an intentionally *multicultural ministry in Spanish.* Particularly in large urban areas, a growing number of people who speak Spanish relate to the Latino community, though their cultural or ethnic background is not Latino. There are already some Spanish-language

109

> As the years go by how will the majority of [Latino] churches identify themselves? Will we see churches that are formed by both immigrants and people of 2nd and 3rd generations? Will we have churches completely of Latino origin of 2nd and 3rd generation but English speaking? Or might it be that the majority of the 2nd and 3rd generation will become part of English-language congregations contributing, in this way, to the diversity of the body of Christ in the context of dominant culture?
>
> SOFÍA HERRERA

churches that have members who are not Latino or Latin American. We need churches that will see this as their ministry and that will begin to develop bridges with other ethnic groups, using Spanish as the principal language of communication.

Already, many Latino churches are bilingual, or translate their services, or have separate services in both languages. Other Latino churches use forms of Spanglish or "Tex-Mex" in their services. We need more churches that will use both languages without formally translating between one and the other. Many Latinos inhabit a linguistic world where they use both languages without thinking about it. It is important to develop religious services, Bible studies, and other programs *without distinguishing languages* that reflect the lived reality of many of our people.

> My conviction is that to struggle for churches to remain "Latino," as other ethnic groups did, is useless. The person that wants to be pure Latino should return to [his] country of origin. One begins to see this in the first generation of Latinos born in the United States. They prefer the English language. If our effort to maintain our culture in a foreign country makes our children leave the church, we have gained nothing. We need to allow things to take their natural course.
>
> JUAN CARLOS ORTIZ

The Latino community also needs experts who will continue analyzing and describing the growing complexities of the Latino community. As we continue seeing variants

110

and differences in the community, we will need to think in new ways to share the good news within the Latino community.

Culture, Language, and Latino Ministry

As previously mentioned, Latinos do not have a single vision of how we should be part of US society. This raises questions about Latino ministry and about the long-term role of the Latino church in the United States.

Some anticipate that the Latino community will structurally assimilate into majority culture. For these people the Latino church is a type of bridge for immigrants while they and their children incorporate fully into majority culture. This type of pastor recognizes that the Latino church plays an important ministry role but is convinced that it will always be among immigrants and that one of its roles is to help immigrants incorporate themselves fully into US society.

> The church that resists accepting the usage of English in its different ministries is destined to lose a generation, particularly when our children, who in spite of following many of our customs and traditions, communicate better in English. Nonetheless, the constant arrival of new Spanish-speaking immigrants, which maintains a significant number of first-generation immigrants, requires that we maintain a balance where we can minister in English or in Spanish. Sadly, to limit the Hispanic church to only Spanish will limit its capacity to extend itself beyond one segment of the community.
>
> JOSÉ GARCÍA

> With respect to languages I believe that we need to struggle to maintain Spanish which is our native language. In church my goal is that the adults learn English and that their children learn Spanish. Our services are in Spanish and sometimes the children of Latino members barely understand Cervantes's language, so I seek for them to learn it. I think we need to live with both languages and even with Spanglish.
>
> LUIS HERNÁNDEZ

111

Others anticipate that there will continue to be a clearly defined Latino reality in the United States over the long term. Latino culture has existed in the United States since the time of the conquest of the Southwest and will continue to exist. For these people there is a Latino subculture that will continue developing its own space in this country. From this perspective, the Latino church is a cultural agent and it should not be afraid of being a part of this process.

Some also anticipate that there will be a need for Latino churches over the long term, even if only because of a constant migration. These people believe that there will be Latinas who will structurally assimilate but that there will always be others who will continue identifying themselves with Latino culture.

Each of these perspectives approaches the issues of culture and language in a different way, particularly in relationship to children and young people. The first are convinced that Spanish and cultural identification are a matter of one or two generations, therefore ministry is done in a cultural and linguistic context in transition. The other two assume a more complex context in which we will continue living between cultures and languages. The principal difference between the last two perspectives just mentioned is their understanding of the role of the church in the matter. Some see that the church should be

> We Latino evangélico Christians are living the fervor of our first love, and that is a flame that does not go out. Latinos have emotional characteristics that make it possible for us to give all for Christ and the ethnic characteristics to go to places where the doors are already closed for Anglo Americans.
>
> ALBERTO MOTTESI

> It is not rare today to hear about Latino missionaries that are having an impact in the world and also that Latin American theology is awakening "gringo" theology. I think that it would even be good to invite "gringo" ministers and members to our services, so that they can feel the "flavor" of the Spirit in our environment.
>
> RENÉ MOLINA

proactive in the process, recognizing its role as a social agent in the United States. Others see Latino churches responding in reaction to what is occurring and not as protagonists in the cultural and linguistic complexity.

It is interesting to note that all of these perspectives assume a medium- or long-term role for the Latino church in the United States. They do not agree on what that role should be, but all recognize that the Latino church has a very important ministry that will continue for an indefinite future.

Beyond the Latino Community

If we Latinos are to be subjects of mission, this means that we need to think about mission beyond the Latino community. Latino *evangélico* churches are also supposed to fulfill the divine mission. Latino churches do not have as many resources, but they have important

> The major challenge for new leaders is to cross ethnic and cultural barriers to develop ministries in which there is an emphasis and vision of the church that is more reflective of the Kingdom.
>
> PABLO ANABALÓN

advantages. One is that we have a strong sense of God's presence and work. As long as we do not forget this, we will avoid the trap of forgetting that the work belongs to God and that we are joining in what God is already doing.

Another advantage is that the work will be done *"desde abajo"* (from the bottom up). Since the mission will not be done from a position of power, there will be less temptation to identify the message of the gospel with

> A resounding Christian leader is one that launches out opening paths in unknown territories, inspiring others to face new challenges and stirring up hope in the midst of fear and discouragement.... We will facilitate and produce opportunities for the "multicultural" and "multiethnic" body of Christ to meet together to worship, interact, and play together in the name of our Lord Jesus Christ.
>
> OSCAR & KARLA GARCÍA

113

the particularities of Latino cultures. The lack of political power also helps us unlink the message of the Kingdom from any specific human political system. Latinas are people who have learned to live among various contexts and in the midst of cultural adaptation. This will facilitate the process of incarnating in other cultural contexts. If we place a missional and transcultural challenge before our bilingual and bicultural young people, we can anticipate that some of them will hear God's call to use what they already have beyond the borders of our community.

A number of immediate opportunities exist for mission beyond the community. In the first place, the Latino community contains several minority groups whose presence has often been completely ignored by Latino churches. Indigenous communities from Latin America have been mistreated in the South and their identity has been ignored and even maligned by some US Latino churches. Also, a number of small ethnic groups from different countries on the continent live in the United States and are unknown by the vast majority of Latinas. Many of these people feel the pain of disdain or the lack of knowledge in the Latino community generally. Our first mission field calls us to repentance and to the divine commitment with the marginalized, forgotten, and oppressed.

> In the past we were peoples that were a mission field. It is encouraging that in the present, thousands of Hispanics who have completed the process of discipleship are becoming a part of the worldwide mission force, by going out and reproducing the ministry of Jesus in other nations of the earth.
>
> JORGE SÁNCHEZ

The majority of Latinos live in communities where there are many people from other ethnic groups, and many live in areas with many cultural mixes.

> We dream that our students and graduates, and also the members of our churches, will be the disciples of the twenty-first century that will "turn the world upside down" for the glory of the Father.
>
> EDUARDO FONT

Latino churches can begin a mission process by building bridges to these communities. Since some Latino congregations own their church buildings or places of worship, they can proactively seek to establish multi-congregational churches in which the resources of the Latino community are used for the benefit of all. They can also develop relationships with other ethnic congregations to respond together to the challenges faced by the whole community.

In many urban centers our young people are interacting and marrying young people from other ethnic groups. Many times the Latino church has assumed that these young people are "lost" to the Latino church. It is time to see them as bridges to develop ministries with a strong multicultural component. Given the flexibility of Latino culture, Latino churches can integrate these people into their congregations and expand their ministry. These marriages can also serve as bridges between congregations of different ethnic backgrounds.

Latino churches also need to be a part of God's mission around the world. Some are already doing it by means of supporting mission projects in Latin America. It is time to make a mission commitment beyond that, and mission projects directed and funded by Latinos are being developed. As these types of commitment continue to grow, we will be able to say, with full integrity, that we are the subjects of mission.[10]

Undetermined Factors

If we take seriously the idea that we live in the midst of discontinuous change, then we have to recognize that we cannot define, beyond the shadow of any doubt, the future of the Latina community in the United States. As has been mentioned several times, everything seems to indicate that the community will continue growing and diversifying. Nonetheless, there are several factors that will probably affect the Latino community and its role in the US context. Reading the signs of the times will mean paying attention to how these (and other) factors evolve.

Situation in Latin America

Latinos in the United States are closely linked to Latin America, as is the rest of the country. Any change in the relationship between the United States and Latin America will have an impact on Latino reality. Particularly, one

> Poor Mexico! So far from God and so close to the United States!
> PORFIRIO DÍAZ

needs to be in touch with political, social, and economic changes in Mexico, Central America, and the Caribbean. Many are anticipating the death of Fidel Castro and the end of the socialist system in Cuba. Any abrupt change will likely create instability on the island and among Cubans in exile. It is also very likely that an event of this type would create a new migratory wave from the island to the United States.

Several Central American countries depend greatly on the money sent home by their citizens in the United States and, to a lesser extent, from other parts of the world. Any change in this arrangement could create instability in Central American countries, which would create more pressure to emigrate to the United States. At this moment, one cannot perceive a solution to the socioeconomic problems of Central America that does not assume a continuation of this bidirectional flow of people and finances between the United States and Central America.

The 2006 presidential elections in Mexico created uncertainty in some segments of the United States because a leftist candidate almost won, and that candidate accused the authorities of manipulating the results so that the right-wing candidate would win. This situation made it clear that relations between the United States and Mexico are key when thinking about the future of the Latino community. Two-thirds of all Latinas in the United States have ties to Mexico (or to the Southwest, which was once a part of Mexico), and it is from Mexico that the largest group of undocumented people immigrates toward the United States. The economies of these two countries are closely linked through the North American Free Trade Agreement

(NAFTA). The border regions of both countries depend directly on the movement of people and commerce in both directions. And much of the popular culture that strengthens Latino identity in this country comes from Mexico.

The political and economic stability or instability of Mexico will affect migratory flows northward. Since several segments of the US economy depend on Mexican immigrant labor, any change in the relationship between these two countries will have a strong impact on both sides of the border and also on the Mexicans and Mexican-Americans in the United States.

We must also be aware of political and economic changes in other parts of Latin America. The United States has served as an escape valve for Latin American instability. Since it is improbable that this relationship between South and North will change, it is very likely that the migratory flow from Latin American countries north will continue with the related implications for the Latino community and for ministry among Latinos.

Changes in Puerto Rico

The political situation in Puerto Rico and its relationship to the United States is unique. The category of Commonwealth (*Estado Libre Asociado*, in Spanish) is used to describe a situation in which Puerto Rico is neither a state, nor a colony, nor an independent country. Puerto Ricans are United States citizens, but they do not have direct representation in Congress, nor can they vote for president. Some have questioned this intermediate status and have worked to change it. But at this moment there does not seem to be clarity about any future different from the present.

Any change in this relationship would have clear implications for the Latino community in the United States. If Puerto Rico were to become a state in the Union, this would probably imply some type of "official" role for the Spanish language, something that would strengthen the use of Spanish throughout the country. On the other hand, if Puerto Rico were to become a country, something that seems highly unlikely, this could affect the legal

117

status of Puerto Ricans who reside in the United States. As long as the current situation between Puerto Rico and the United States continues, one can expect a constant movement of people from the island.

Changes in Immigration Laws

As this book was being written, a debate about an immigration reform law in the United States was taking place. One of the proposals that has been considered would include legalization of the undocumented who are already in the country, a plan for guest workers, and money to attempt to close the border and limit the flow of immigrants in the future. Some people are considering a change in the norms used to decide who has the right to obtain residency or a work visa in this country.

> There will always be a constant flow of recent arrivals here, in spite of the present "noise." This provides the opportunity to continue planting more churches and to expand the growth of the kingdom among Hispanics.
>
> JORGE SÁNCHEZ

No matter how the issue is resolved, one thing is sure; any changes in immigration laws will affect the Latino community. If an anti-immigrant spirit prevails, Latino churches could see themselves adversely affected. This spirit would likely be directed against Latino institutions, particularly those that use the Spanish language. But even if that type of reaction does not occur, Latino churches would find themselves with the dilemma of how to minister to undocumented people who are already part of their churches, or those who would arrive looking for help. The churches would need to decide whether to potentially break the law to help their people or to refuse to help and thereby avoid legal problems but not serve that segment of the community.

On the other hand, if the undocumented were legalized, and a guest worker program was established, this would open a new area of ministry for the churches. After the amnesty of 1986, many churches helped the undocumented put their applications and paperwork in order, something they would probably do again. The churches would also need to think about their ministry toward those who would come to this country with temporary work visas from Latin America.

But if the situation continues as is, without a resolution for the undocumented population, this implies another type of ministry among people who live in the shadows and in fear. One can anticipate that this issue will continue being debated far beyond the approval of any specific law. The work of Latino churches will be affected no matter which direction the country takes in relationship to this matter.

Massive Migration from Another Context

At the moment the largest migration flow toward the United States is from Latin America. If current laws or migratory patterns change, this would also affect intercultural relations and the role of the Latino community in this country. Changes in global commercial patterns could create changes in migratory patterns, particularly from Asia. If there were to be significant migratory changes, this would imply missional changes for the Latino church.

Strong Anti-Latino Reactions

The relations between the Latino community and the majority population in this country have always been complex. In the last few years, the majority population has taken several steps to "limit" Latino cultural influence that is seen, by some, as a threat to majority culture. Laws against bilingual education, against the use of Spanish in public spaces, against the rights of the undocumented, against the usage of social services by those who are not citizens, and other similar laws, have been passed.

But the influence of Latino culture in the United States keeps growing. Latino subcultures are influencing majority culture and not only being changed by the majority. There is also a growth of interest among non-Latinos in things Latino. It is yet to be seen whether anti-Latino attitudes change to the point of **119** creating a strong reaction against the Latino community. If that happens, the churches will find it necessary to respond to that challenge. On the other hand, Latino churches can be proactive in building bridges with the majority community to create a more positive environment among our communities.

Acceptance of Spanish

The United States does not have a single perspective on the role of Spanish in national life. On the one hand, the use of the language continues to grow. Spanish-language mass media has a growing influence throughout the country, and these media are receiving the investment of those who hope to have an impact in the growing Latino market.

At the same time there are several efforts to limit the place of Spanish in public life, including attempts to declare English the official language of the country. It is yet to be seen whether Latinos will take steps together to defend a role for Spanish in the life of the community. Also, it is not clear what place a dialect of Spanish, such as Spanglish, might have. At this moment one sees a growth in the usage of Spanish. The growth or decline of its usage will affect the ministry of the Latino church.[11]

Influence of Latino Youth Subcultures

Many Latino young people are supporting popular Latino culture. They are listening to music in Spanish by Latino artists and they are attending their concerts. The market for Latino cultural production and for popular culture in Spanish is growing. Of course, Latina young people are also supporting popular culture in English and the cultural influences of other minority groups. If young people continue identifying themselves with popular Latino culture, this will serve as the basis for the growth of its influence and the place of things Latino in the national environment. On the other hand, if Latino young people were to reject Latino culture, this could have serious implications for the future of Latino identity in the country.

120

None of the factors that we have described will bring fundamental changes in Latino reality by themselves. But each can serve as a possible sign of changes in the air. A profound change in a combination of these factors could affect Latino ministry and Latino identity in the United States over the long term. Latino pastors and leaders will need to be attentive to these changes so that they can respond effectively to the realities of the community.

6

Dreams and Visions

The Latino *evangélico* church has an important future in the United States. It has a role to play in the midst of the massive changes that are occurring in our country. One of the ways to think and dream about this future is through metaphors and images that help us reflect on the fulfillment of its mission in the Latino community and beyond. Each of these images points toward a key aspect of how the Latino church can be what God wants. They also encourage us to consider the role of the Latino *evangélico* church in the divine project around the world.

> We understand that God has brought the Latino people to the United States of North America with a redemptive purpose. The Latino community not only comes to model to a country in moral and spiritual decadence the family and religious values that distinguish us, but also as a reminder to the people of their greed and tendency to oppression, and to force them to re-examine their own ethnocentrism.
>
> ROBERTO COLÓN

Images of the Latino Church in Mission

Latino churches are growing in their commitment toward God's mission. We continue broadening our understanding of what God wants from us within the Latino community, in US society, and in the world. Each of these images points toward a key truth of what we can be for the glory of God in Jesus Christ.

Community/Family

A crucial need in the community is community and family support. We live in an individualistic society, and many of our people are getting lost in this context. God has not called us to walk alone, and the attempts to do so are producing a great deal of personal and social harm.

Many Latino churches have grasped the concept of the church as family or community. These churches are places where people who are far from families and communities can find support and relationships. These churches serve as a point of encounter and a place where needy people can find help for spiritual, social, physical, and emotional needs. And these churches are also working to walk with broken families and to strengthen families that are working well.

> I believe that the progress of the Hispanic church in the United States will depend on a premeditated and intentional effort to study and prepare ourselves to imitate Christ, "[who] emptied himself, taking the form of a slave, being born in human likeness" (Philippians 2:7).
>
> JOSÉ GARCÍA

What is important is to take this concept to a higher level. We need to use this image to strengthen the concept of mutual commitment, where we support each other on the road of life toward the eternal Kingdom. The community needs to be the place of encounter and connection, and also of interpretation. It needs to be a place where we feel supported and also where we have the space and liberty to grow toward all that God wants for each member.

The communities also need a countercultural sense. We need to proclaim the values of the Kingdom, values that will put us in tension with a society that promotes individualism and privatization. We need to form people with a clear sense

124

of who they are before God, but also knowing that they can serve others as Christ did. We need to form people who will be a part of a transformative community, a family that calls society to transformation in Christ and that seeks to be a part of the divine transformation in our society. These traditional Latino values of family and community offer hope to many people who feel alone

> It is said that missionaries no longer come from the first world; they arrive in the first world. The first world is becoming lost, swallowed up by the materialism and greed that have terrible consequences for the vulnerable, the little ones who incarnate Christ. The missionaries of the third world (and their children and grandchildren who remember their stories) have a prophetic mission to awake the first world to spiritual realities and eternal values.
>
> ALEXIA SALVATIERRA

and lost. They also offer an alternative to those people trapped in the culture of individualistic consumption. We need to teach and practice an alternative that emphasizes divine values and the fact that material things and greed are not the most important things in life. The church as community and family presents an image of what the church can and should be in the world. The Latino church can be an important part of fomenting an alternative vision in our society.

Bridge

The principal function of a bridge is to connect so that there can be movement in two directions. The Latino church can visualize its mission in terms of a bridge, first between God and humanity. We have the message of hope in Jesus Christ, a message that offers a future and a reestablished relationship with God. We need to proclaim the message of hope and conversion with courage among so many who urgently need the touch of our God.

But this message of reconciliation and relationship also can be applied to human relations. The Latino church can be a bridge for Latino young people confused about their identity

125

and their relationship with majority culture. As previously mentioned, the church has the potential for serving its young people so that they can strengthen their identity as Latino believers even as they cross bridges between their polycentric identities to respond to the future with hope.

A bridge Latina church can help people walk between Latino cultures and the other cultures of this country in an environment of security and accompaniment. We have the connections with sisters and brothers in churches of other cultures. We can dream of Latino churches that consciously seek to be bridges, creating relationships of confidence with other churches in which people can cross back and forth, celebrating our differences and seeking to create bridges of unity.

> I would like to dream with a Latino church that educates and loves its young people, trains leaders for the future, and maintains and shares its culture, not because of pride, but because it is something good that it has to share.
>
> DANNY MARTÍNEZ

The Latino church can also be a bridge of reconciliation between some of our Latin American peoples that have centuries-old antagonisms. It is here in the United States that many Latinas are "discovering" these injustices against native peoples and the marginalization of many people in Latin America. The church can be a bridge of reconciliation between people here. But it can also make part of its mission to be a bridge among alienated peoples on the whole continent.

The church can also work to create bridges between Latino communities and other minority groups in this country. Many of our churches, particularly in urban areas, are in places of increased racial tensions. If we have the vision of being a bridge, we can create relations with churches and leaders in our communities to foster better relations between the various ethnic communities in our neighborhoods.

A final important bridge that needs to be strengthened is between the United States and Latin America. The future of the countries on the continent is linked together. Latino believers **126** who have a foot in each area can serve as bridges to address historical problems and the misunderstandings that have become a "normal" part of regional relations. On each side of the Río Grande River (or Río Bravo) there are biased attitudes and perspectives that limit the possibility of creating the type of relationships that can help us walk together toward the future. Latino believers are well prepared to serve as interpreters of reality so that both sides can better understand the hopes and fears of our peoples in the North and the South.

Propellant

US society has limited and cloistered the place of many Latinos. Many women have lived the limitations of a context that closes off opportunities, both because they are women and because they are Latina. We can also point to how our society cloisters the opportunities of people with little formal education, the undocumented, and many others. The church can serve as a propulsion rocket that propels these people toward new opportunities and hopes.

> We think that the Latino community has a principal place in the redemptive plan, since this is a marginalized and oppressed community. It is in this context that the program described by our Lord Jesus Christ in Luke 4:18-19 becomes more relevant.
> SAÚL & ROSAMARÍA MALDONADO

On the one hand, churches can continue opening spaces within ministries and in leadership. Our people need opportunities where they can develop as people and as leaders. US society will often tend to close spaces, instead of opening them. As they serve other people in the church, our cloistered people gain the confidence and self-esteem necessary to be able to open spaces in other areas of their lives. The churches can also be places that encourage the development of people, that provide spaces to learn and develop, and that seek out opportunities to do this. The churches can also provide service opportunities for people whose gifts and capacities are ignored in other contexts.

127

The Latino church can also take this perspective in relationship to its young people. If the churches will take seriously the task described in the last chapter, they will approach youth ministry with the perspective that it is our task to form, disciple, and propel our young people toward the future that God has for them in this country or beyond.

> The Latino is designed to cross cultural boundaries, so he therefore is one of the peoples blessed for missionary work, be it national or international. The Latino is not only an economic gift to this society, she can also be the leaven sent to other communities of this great nation to leaven them with the gospel of Jesus Christ.
>
> EDUARDO FONT

A very specific type of propulsion that the Latino church can fulfill is the sending of missionaries, pastors, and workers to the world. The young people in Latino churches have key cultural and linguistic tools, since many are already bilingual and know how to live and work in a multicultural environment. They have developed in churches that have a strong sense of the presence and work of God. Since they grew up in churches that have always been on the margins, it will be much easier for Latina missionaries to do mission *"desde abajo"* [from the bottom up] as previously described. We need to identify and encourage a new generation of Latino missionaries to work among our people and beyond, in the whole gamut of God's mission in the world.

> Our challenge has to do with the totality of human society; this includes the arts, politics, education, sports, and the mass media. We need to send our young people to the best universities of the country and completely participate in the dynamic process of this multiethnic country.
>
> ALBERTO MOTTESI

Change Agents

Many Latinos have lived our lives with a certain fatalistic tendency. We have often heard friends or relatives say *"así lo quiso*

Dios" [that is the way God wanted it] as a way of merely reacting to what has happened. Those of us who have taken this perspective have not felt responsible or seen ourselves as agents in our world.

The gospel invites us to create another important image in the Latino church, that of change agent. We are part of our world and God calls us to seek change in people, families, relationships, and in our society in general. Our growth implies increased responsibility in our community, our country, and our world. We want to recognize the importance of this role and be agents of the change God wants to bring to the world.

The Latino Churches of the Future

It is clear that the Latino *evangélico* churches of the future will continue diversifying. The needs of our people and our world demand a variety of models and visions in relationship to the ministry of the church. Each new generation of Latino pastors and leaders is dreaming and walking in various directions at the same time. Latino churches will continue growing, as will ministries from the Latino community that go beyond the community. The number of Latinos who will be an active part of non-Latino churches will also continue to grow. Each new challenge will propel people to think in new ways about what Latino ministry is and how to be faithful to God's mission in the world.

Our Place in the Divine Vision

It is clear that it is time for Latino churches to look beyond the community, to take responsibility as a part of the world in which God has placed us. This implies analyzing the role that we should play in the Latino community

> The arrival of Latinos to the United States is something sovereign done by God.
>
> JIM TOLLE

and in US society. Our churches need to reflect on the impact **129** we should have on US churches in general, in majority society, and among other minority groups in the country. We need to share the gospel, once again, with people who have forgotten it. We also need to invite our sisters and brothers in other cultures to question and seek to change those aspects of US culture that reflect death instead of life. God calls us to be a bridge and an agent of transformation in this country starting from our *mestizo* reality.

> I believe in the role of Latinos as missionaries outside of their culture. It is the Latino's time to take the Word of God to the entire world and to all cultures.
>
> SERGIO NAVARRETE

We also need to widen the vision of our role in Latin America and in our globalized world. Today there are Latinos and Latin Americans in many countries around the world. We should not see this as a mere coincidence but rather as an opportunity that God opens up to us to join in what God is doing in the world. God invites us to minister from the place where we are today and to then go far beyond, toward the future God has for all humanity.

Toward the Unity of the Church

Throughout this book, we have spoken of Latino reality and of the ministry of the Latino church. But we must never lose sight of the fact that God calls us to reflect the unity of the church with our sisters and brothers of the cultures of our world. Our great new challenge will be to find new models of ministry that reflect the unity of the church in the midst of the diversity that is human reality created by God. The answer is not to impose one culture on the rest, nor is it to have a model of church that justifies human divisions. What we seek are models of transformation that can be a testimony to the world of what God seeks for all humanity.

After this I looked, and there was a great multitude that no one could count, from every nation, from all tribes and peoples and languages, standing before the throne and before the Lamb, robed in white, with palm branches in their hands. They cried out in a loud voice, saying, "Salvation belongs to our God who is seated on the throne, and to the Lamb!" (Rev 7:9-10)

This passage presents the divine vision of unity in diversity. The Latino *evangélico* church is a small reflection of this, a place where we see flashes of God's future. We continue walking toward that vision in which from our Latino reality we can join with others and together celebrate the unity that God is creating in Christ, through the power of the Holy Spirit that is working through the church in the world. We continue in hope toward that future.

APPENDIX A

Resources for Latino Ministry

What follows is a list of resources that can be of help in ministry in the Latino community. It is not meant to be exhaustive but merely to provide a list of sources that can be helpful.

Previous Books about Ministry in the Latino Community

Several books about Latino ministry in the United States have been published. Three of the ones that have had the most circulation have been, in order of publication:

Los Hispanos en los Estados Unidos. Un reto y una oportunidad para la iglesia by José Reyes (Cleveland, Tenn.: White Wing Publishing House and Press, 1985).
Hispanic Ministry in North America by Alex Montoya (Grand Rapids, Mich.: Zondervan Publishing House, 1987).
The Hispanic Challenge Opportunities Confronting the Church by Manuel Ortiz (Downers Grove, Ill.: InterVarsity Press, 1993).

Various denominations and movements have published literature about Latino ministry, particularly for their specific needs. This material can be found through the various denominational offices. There are also a number of websites that focus on specific aspects of ministry among Latinos.

Studies of Latino Churches in the United States

To this date, a history of Latino *evangélico* churches in the United States has not been written. A preliminary effort was published as a project of CEHILA (Comisión de Estudios de Historia de la Iglesia en Latinoamérica y el Caribe [Commission for Historical Studies of the Church in Latin America and the Caribbean]) USA.

Iglesias peregrinas en busca de identidad Cuadros del protestantismo latino en los Estados Unidos edited by Juan Francisco Martínez and Luis Scott (Buenos Aires: Kairós, 2004).

Denomination histories, regional studies, and even studies on specific time periods have been written. Here is an introductory selection:

Avance: A Vision for a New Mañana by Johnny Ramírez-Johnson, Edwin Hernández, et al. (Loma Linda, Calif.: Loma Linda University Press, 2003).

Each in Our Own Tongue: A History of Hispanics in United Methodism edited by Justo González (Nashville: Abingdon Press, 1991).

Hacia una historia de la iglesia evangélica hispana de California del Sur edited by Rodelo Wilson (Austin: AEHT, 1993).

Hidden Stories: Unveiling the History of the Latino Church edited by Daniel Rodríguez and David Cortés-Fuentes (AETH, 1994).

Hispanic Methodists, Presbyterians, and Baptists in Texas by Paul Barton (Austin: University of Texas Press, 2006).

Iglesia Presbiteriana: A History of Presbyterians and Mexican Americans in the Southwest by R. Douglas Brackenridge and Francisco O. García-Treto (San Antonio: Trinity University Press, 1974).

Latino Churches: Faith, Family, and Ethnicity in the Second Generation by Ken Crane (El Paso: LFB Scholarly Publishing, 2003).

134

Latino Pentecostal Identity: Evangelical Faith, Self, and Society by
   Arlene Sánchez-Walsh (New York: Columbia University Press,
   2003).
Of Borders and Margins: Hispanic Disciples in Texas, 1888-1945
   by Daisy Machado (New York: Oxford University Press,
   2003).
*Protestantes/Protestants: Hispanic Christianity within Mainline
   Traditions* edited by David Maldonado (Nashville:
   Abingdon Press, 1999)
Protestantism in the Sangre de Cristos by Randi Jones Walker
   (Albuquerque: University of New Mexico Press, 1991).
*Sea la Luz: The Making of Mexican Protestantism in the American
   Southwest, 1829–1900* by Juan Francisco Martínez (Denton:
   University of North Texas Press, 2006).

One can also find denominational studies of limited circulation. Generally, these studies can only be found through the
offices of each particular denomination.

Information about Latinos in the United States

American Immigration Law Foundation (ailf.org)
   This organization addresses issues related to immigration.
They publish studies on migration and immigration reform as
part of their Immigration Policy Center.

Institute for the Study of Latino Religion (nd.edu/~cslr)
   This Institute of the University of Notre Dame studies vari-
ous aspects of Latino religion and the role of theological edu-
cation in the formation of Latino religious leaders. The
Hispanic Church Research Initiative is sponsored by Pew
Charitable Trusts.

League of United Latin American Citizens (lulac.org)
   This is one of the oldest Latino organizations in the country.
Their website includes information on issues of interest to the
Latino community at a national level and links to many other
organizations that support Latinos. They offer opportunities

135

for citizen participation in issues having an impact on the community. (There are many good organizations of this type in the country. This one is used as a sample of many others that can be of help.)

Pew Hispanic Center (pewhispanic.org)
This center has developed and published many studies on Latino reality in the United States, including the studies on its religious tendencies and on the usage of English and Spanish that were quoted in the book.

United States Census Bureau (census.gov)
The office of the Census has developed a series of specific studies on Latinos in the United States. When this book was being written, the most up-to-date studies were based on estimates that the census had done through 2004. See census.gov/popu-lation/www/socdemo/hispanic/cps2004.html. The Census Bu-reau updates its information regularly.

History of Latinos in the United States

Several books are available on the history of Latinos in the United States. This book specifically refers to:

Harvest of Empire: A History of Latinos in America by Juan Gonzá-lez (New York: Penguin Books, 2001).

Other books that can be helpful in understanding the history of Latinos in the United States are:

The Columbia History of Latinos in the United States Since 1960 by David Gutiérrez (New York: Columbia University Press, 2006).
Everything You Need to Know about Latino History by Himilce Novas (New York: Plume, 2007).
Latino USA: A Cartoon History by Ilan Stavans and Lalo Alcaraz (New York: Basic Books, 2000).

Latino Theology

There is an extensive bibliography of books written on Latino theology in the United States. The five included here are samples, including an introductory text, two books on Latino theology written by very well-known authors in the Latino *evangélico* community, and two works of *"teología en conjunto,"* projects written in collaboration that demonstrate the Latino effort to work together.

Introducing Latino/a Theologies by Miguel de la Torre and Edwin Aponte (Maryknoll, N.Y.: Orbis Books, 2001).
The Liberating Spirit: Toward an Hispanic American Pentecostal Social Ethic by Eldín Villafañe (Grand Rapids, Mich.: Eerdmans, 1994).
Mañana: Christian Theology from a Hispanic Perspective by Justo González (Nashville: Abingdon Press, 1990).
Handbook of Latino/a Theologies, edited by Miguel de la Torre and Edwin Aponte (St. Louis: Chalice Press, 2006).
Teología en Conjunto: A Collaborative Hispanic Protestant Theology, edited by José David Rodríguez and Loida Martell-Otero (Louisville: Westminster John Knox Press, 1997).

Youth Ministry

Being Latino in Christ: Finding Wholeness in your Ethnic Identity by Orlando Crespo (Downers Grove, Ill.: InterVarsity Press, 2003).
This book was written for Latino young people struggling to develop their identity as Latinos and as Christians.

Especialidades juveniles – USA (especialidadesjuveniles.com/ especialidades_usa.shtm)
Includes materials, activities, and other resources for the person working with Latino young people in the United States. This project is a part of Especialidades Juveniles for Latin America. This is a project of Youth Specialties.

137

Instituto Fe y Vida (feyvida.org/esp/index.html)

A Catholic organization that studies Latino young people and produces materials for Latino youth pastoral work. It includes many resources for the person who wants to better understand the complexity of ministering among Latino youth in the United States.

Multicultural Churches and Ministries

This book did not address the topic of multicultural ministries directly, though it recognized that almost every Latino church in the United States has to be multicultural to be able to minister effectively within the Latino community and beyond. Some of the books written on the possibilities and the complexities of multicultural ministry in the United States are:

Crossing the Ethnic Divide: The Multiethnic Church on a Mission by Kathleen Garces-Foley (New York: Oxford University Press, 2007).

Divided by Faith: Evangelical Religion and the Problem of Race in America by Michael Emerson and Christian Smith (New York: Oxford University Press, 2000).

One New People: Models for Developing a Multiethnic Church by Manuel Ortiz (Downers Grove, Ill.: InterVarsity Press, 1996).

People of the Dream: Multiracial Congregations in the United States by Michael Emerson and Rodney Woo (Princeton: Princeton University Press, 2006).

United by Faith: The Multiracial Congregation as an Answer to the Problem of Race by Curtiss DeYoung, Michael Emerson, George Yancey, and Karen Kim (New York: Oxford University Press, 2003).

The Wolf Shall Dwell with the Lamb: A Spirituality for Leadership in a Multicultural Community by Eric Law (Atlanta: Chalice Press, 1993).

APPENDIX B

Persons Interviewed for This Book

Pablo Anabalón—Pastor, Iglesia del Pacto Evangélico, Eagle Rock, California

David Castro—International Executive Director of Victory Education and Training Institute and pastor of Victory Outreach Church, Riverside, California

Clementina Chacón—Associate Pastor, Iglesia de la Comunidad, Iglesia Presbiteriana USA (PCUSA), Highland Park, California

Roberto Colón—Pastor, Iglesia de la Comunidad, Iglesia Presbiteriana USA (PCUSA), Highland Park, California

Walter Contreras—Former Director of Church Planting, Current Director of Mobilization and Connections for the Department of World Mission, Evangelical Covenant Church.

Eduardo Font—Founding President of Escuela de Evangelistas Alberto Mottesi and Pastor of Iglesia Esperanza Viva, Orange, California

José García—Bishop, State Supervisor of Latino Churches in California, Church of God of the Prophecy

Oscar and Karla García—Regional minister, church planters of Latino churches, American Baptist Churches

Adelita Garza—Pastor, Ministerios Puente, Assemblies of God, Ventura, California

María Hamilton—Pastor, Misión Hispana Bíblica and Executive Director of Simi Valley Community Care Center, United Methodist Church, Simi Valley, California

Luís Hernández—Church planter and pastor of Iglesia Misionera Nueva Visión, Moreno Valley, CA and La Cosecha – Nuevo Comienzo, La Puente, California, Assemblies of God

Sofía Herrera—Director of Community Psychology, Institute for Urban Initiatives, Fuller Theological Seminary and candidate to the priesthood, Episcopal Church, Diocese of Los Angeles, California

Saúl and Rosamaría Maldonado—Pastors, Ministerios Betel, American Baptist Churches, Pasadena, California

Danny Martínez—Pastor, Church of the Redeemer, Evangelical Covenant Church, Los Angeles, California

René Molina—General Pastor, Iglesias de Restauración, ELIM, Los Angeles, California

Alberto Mottesi—International Evangelist and Conference speaker

Sergio Navarrete—Superintendent, Southern Pacific Latin American District, Assemblies of God, La Puente, CA

James Ortiz—Pastor, My Friend's Place, Assemblies of God, Whittier, California

140

Juan Carlos Ortiz—Pastor Emeritus, Hispanic Department, Crystal Cathedral, Garden Grove, California

Alexia Salvatierra—Pastor, Evangelical Lutheran Church in America and Executive Director of CLUE (Clergy and Laity United for Economic Justice)

Jorge Sánchez—Pastor, Comunidad de las Américas, Pasadena, California

Fernando Santillana—Former Director of Latino Ministries – California Pacific Annual Conference, United Methodist Church; current pastor of the United Methodist Church, Norwalk, California

Jim "Jaime" Tolle—Pastor de Iglesia en el Camino / Church on the Way; Supervisor of Foursquare Churches, Van Nuys, California

Maribel Zacapa—Pastor, Iglesia de Dios de la Profecía, Lompoc, California

Notes

Introduction

1. Because of time and space limitations, I decided to only include leaders from southern California. The Latino community in southern California is the largest in the United States and has certain distinctions that do not exist in other parts of the country. Nevertheless, by limiting the interviews to leaders from this region, I recognize that the book cannot reflect all of the cultural and ministry varieties that are particular to other regions of the United States.

2. In many parts of the Spanish-speaking world, including Spain, *evangélico* has been used practically as a synonym for *Protestant*. Among Latinos in the United States, its usage is more complex. Some use the English terms (*evangelical, mainline y pentecostal*), even though these divisions do not always fit among Latino churches and they separate people who potentially would walk together in Latin America. When AMEN (Alianza Ministerial Evangélica Naciona—National Evangélico Ministerial Alliance) was formed, the members wanted to use evangélico in the broader sense, though this created some confusion for those who wanted *evangélico* to be an exact translation of *evangelical*. It is probable that the term *evangélico* will continue being used in both ways within the Spanish-speaking-community.

3. This book is being published simultaneously in Spanish and English.

1. The Complexities of Our Latina Reality

1. See the book *Hispanic/Latino Identity: A Philosophical Perspective*, by Jorge Gracia (Malden, Mass.: Blackwell Publishers, 1999), for a discussion of the issue. It includes a good description of the usage of each term.

2. Throughout the book I will be using the term *Latino*, recognizing that there are people like Jorge Gracia (see note 1) who insist that we must use *Hispanic*. This preference reflects the common usage both terms have in southern California.

3. These numbers come from the US Census Bureau report for 2004. "Other"

includes Dominicans and Latinos who do not identify with any national background. Some of the descendants of the conquered also mark "other" because they do not see themselves identified under any other category.

4. Central and South Americans have not migrated to specific areas of the United States as much as other Latino groups.

5. See Juan González, *Harvest of Empire: A History of Latinos in America* (New York: Viking, 2000) for a historical review of how different Latino groups became a part of the United States.

6. Telling the stories of these communities also implies questioning the popular US understanding that sees all Latinos as immigrants or descendants of immigrants.

7. In other words, the majority of Latinos spend our time "negotiating" the various cultural options, be they Latino, from majority society, or from other cultural minorities in the country. To be polycentric means that one does not assimilate into any one culture, but that one learns to live among several changing focuses, depending on the needs of the moment.

8. Orlando Crespo proposes another way to describe Latino identity between majority culture and Latino culture in his book *Being Latino in Christ: Finding Wholeness in Your Ethnic Identity* (Downers Grove, Ill.: InterVarsity Press, 2003).

9. The lyrics of "Más allá de México" (Beyond Mexico) are based on the old Spanish language hymn "Más allá del sol" (Beyond the Sun) and was written by a group of students from the Baptist Seminary of Santa Ana, El Salvador, in 1993. The chorus lyrics are "Más allá de México / yo tengo un hogar, hogar bello hogar, más allá de México" (Beyond México / I have a home, home sweet home, beyond Mexico). They wrote three stanzas that follow the same idea based on the original stanzas of the hymn.

10. See *Harvest of Empire*.

11. India María is a popular Mexican comic who made a comedy about the Mexican immigrant experience called *Ni de aquí, ni de allá* (Neither from Here, Nor from There).

12. This is Samuel Huntington's argument in his book *We Are We? The Challenges to America's National Identity* (New York: Simon & Schuster, 2004).

13. Ilan Stavans, *The Hispanic Condition: The Power of a People* (New York: Harper Perennial, 2nd Edition, 2001). See also *Living in Spanglish: The Search for Latino Identity in America*, by Ed Morales (New York: St. Martin's, 2002).

2. Protestants and Latinos in the United States

1. See *Sea la Luz: The Making of Mexican Protestantism in the American Southwest, 1829-1900* (Juan Francisco Martínez, University of North Texas Press, 2006) for a description of Protestant evangelization among the Mexicans who stayed in the Southwest after the United States took it from Mexico in 1848.

144

2. When the Alianza de Ministerios Evangélicos Nacionales (AMEN) was formed, it had problems with some "evangelical" organizations in the United States because the latter wanted AMEN to only include "evangelicals" and not all Latinos who consider themselves *evangélicos*.

3. Second and third stanzas of "Hay una senda" (There Is but One Way) by Robert C. Savage. The translation is:

> My friends and all my relatives
> Those with whom I had a relationship
> Hated me because of His name
> When they learned that I gave myself to Christ.
>
> That way of much suffering
> The way that heaven prepared for me
> Was transformed in the happy moment
> When my Christ called me to heaven.

4. See, for example, the documents of the May 2007 Latin American bishop's conference (CELAM V) and the declarations of Pope Benedict XVI in which there are several references to "the sects" when speaking of the protestants or the neo-Pentecostal movements that are growing in Latin America (http://www.celam.info/content/section/14/332/).

3. Resources within the Latino Community and Church

1. Linda Chávez proposes this perspective in her book *Out of the Barrio: Toward a New Politics of Hispanic Assimilation* (New York: Basic Books, 1992).

2. The 2003 study can be found at http://www.nd.edu/~cslr/. The second report (2007) can be found at http://pewforum.org/surveys/hispanic/. The second study was published while this book was being written. The results had still not been analyzed in depth when the manuscript was sent to the publisher.

3. See the explanation describing the term *evangélico* in the introduction and in the previous chapter.

4. For more information, see the bibliography at the end of the book.

5. See Justo González' *Santa Biblia: The Bible Through Hispanic Eyes* (Nashville: Abingdon Press, 1996).

6. Roberto Goizueta describes this space as the *locus theologicius*, the place where we should do our theological reflection. See *Caminemos con Jesús: Toward a Hispanic/Latino Theology of Accompaniment* (Maryknoll, N.Y.: Orbis Books, 1995), particularly chapter seven.

7. Ortiz, Manuel, *Hispanic Challenge Opportunities Confronting the Church* (Downers Grove, Ill.: InterVarsity Press, 1993), 104–5.

8. Justo González suggests that mestizaje is one of five particular perspectives that Latinos have as they approach the interpretation of the Bible. The

145

others are marginality, poverty, exile, and solidarity. See *Santa Biblia*.

9. *American Immigration Law Foundation* (www.immigrationpolicy.org) has published several studies on the impact of undocumented immigration on the national economy. They have concluded that the undocumented contribute to the national economy in various ways. For example, see the study "Immirants, Skills, and Wages: Measuring the Economic Gains from Immigration," by Giovanni Peri in *Immigration Policy in Focus* (Vol. 5, No. 3, March 2006).

4. What Latino Churches Are Doing

1. As the differences between segments of the Latino community keep growing, it is yet to be seen what specific terms will develop to name these differences. In other words, will the terms *Latino or Hispanic* continue being sufficiently useful to describe this diversity?

2. In his book *One New People: Models for Developing a Multiethnic Church* (Downers Grove, Ill.: InterVarsity Press, 1996) Manuel Ortiz describes the different ways that one can be involved in multiethnic ministry. He describes multi-congregational and multicultural models of doing church.

3. This model is being celebrated in several circles, though it represents a very small percentage of churches in the Latino community. Appendix A includes a list of books related to intercultural ministry in the United States.

4. Jonathan Bonk describes the problems that arise when money has so much influence on missionary work in *Missions and Money: Affluence as a Western Missionary Problem* (Maryknoll, N.Y.: Orbis Books, 1991).

5. Ministering for Today and for Tomorrow

1. It is important to take into account the differences in terms used in the Spanish-speaking world to youth ministry. Generally, *ministerio juvenil* in Spanish refers to what in English is called *young adult ministry*, and what is called *youth ministry* in English is adolescent ministry in Spanish. These divisions are not clearcut since there are different educational systems in the United States and in Latin America, but it is important to recognize that *youth group* and *pastoral juvenil* do not necessarily refer to ministry among people of the same age.

2. The categories used in this diagram were developed by Instituto Fe y Vida. See *The Status of Hispanic Youth and Young Adult Ministry in the United States: A Preliminary Study*, by Ken Johnson-Mondragón (Stockton, Calif.: Instituto Fe y Vida, 2002).

3. It is important to note the observation made by many people that there is a fundamental linguistic difference between the immigrant generation and each succeeding generation. The struggle of the first group is to learn English; the struggle of every succeeding generation is to not forget Spanish.

146

Many immigrant parents assume that their children will have the same problems as they had, and so they speak to them in English, even if badly spoken, not wanting their children to suffer as they did. They do not realize that their children are losing a key opportunity to not forget Spanish.

4. Samuel Huntington, professor at Harvard University, presents the perspective that Latinos pose a threat to national identity in his book *Who Are We? The Challenges to America's National Identity* (New York: Simon & Schuster, 2004).

5. Orlando Crespo wrote his excellent book, *Being Latino in Christ: Finding Wholeness in Your Ethnic Identity* (Downers Grove, Ill.: InterVarsity Press, 2003), for Latino young people who are trying to affirm their Christian and Latino identity.

6. Elizabeth Conde-Frazier studied Latino Bible Institutes, demonstrating the importance of these institutions for the formation of pastors and leaders in the Latino community. See *Hispanic Bible Institutes: A Community of Theological Construction* (University of Scranton Press, 2004).

7. There are also other problems when trying to recognize studies done in seminaries or Bible Institutes in Latin America. First of all, the majority of Bible Institutes and seminaries in Latin America are not formally accredited because accreditation is done by ministries of education in most countries and many of these do not accredit theology programs. But even accredited programs present problems because the first theological degree accredited in Latin America is a *licenciatura* (roughly equivalent to a B.A.), while in the United States it is a master's degree. For issues of ordination, a *licenciatura* in Latin America counts the same as a master of divinity, but they do not have equal weight when dealing with the transfer of degrees and academic units.

8. According to the ATS (Association of Theological Schools) report, during academic year 2006–2007 there were 3,104 Latino students in ATS member institutions (ats.edu/Resources/FactBook/2007/2006-07%20Annual%20 Data%20Tables.pdf). They constituted 3.8 percent of the total of 81,063 students. This includes students from institutions in Puerto Rico and Canada, so the actual percentage of Latino and Latina students in the United States is not exact.

9. Several seminaries and Christian universities are working with Latino Bible Institutes to create spaces for them within accredited programs. For example, in southern California, Vanguard University of the Assemblies of God has an agreement with Latin American Bible Institute (LABI) and with Latin American Theological Seminary (LATS) to allow their students to continue their studies at the University. Haggard School of Theology of Azusa Pacific University has an arrangement with Facultad de Teología (Theological Faculty) of the Foursquare Church to accept their graduates in their master's programs. Fuller Theological Seminary works with these Bible Institutes and also with Centro Hispano de Estudios Teológicos (CHET) (Hispanic Center of Theological Studies) to receive their graduates in master's programs.

147

10. COMINHA (Cooperación Misionera de Hispanos de Norteamérica) (Hispanic Missionary Cooperation in North America), a part of COMIBAM (Cooperación Misionera Iberoamericana) (Iberoamerican Missionary Cooperation), is an initial effort to participate with churches in Latin America and Spain in world mission.

11. The data on the usage of Spanish among Latinos provides contradictory information. On the one hand, the results of the US Census Bureau report a growth in the usage of the Spanish language. Tied to this is the growth of the Spanish-language mass media. On the other hand, studies on the usage of Spanish among Latinos seem to indicate that the vast majority of Latinos quit using the language after two generations in the United States. See the Pew study on *"Bilingualism,"* published in March 2004 (pewhispanic.org/files/factsheets/12.pdf) for an analysis of the changes occurring in the usage of the Spanish language among Latinos.

148